A VICTORIAN FAMILY
1870–1900

*Interior, Morning, by Patrick William Adam*

# A VICTORIAN FAMILY

## 1870–1900

## MOLLY HUGHES

Sidgwick & Jackson
London

This abridged edition first published
in Great Britain 1990 by
Sidgwick & Jackson Limited
1 Tavistock Chambers, Bloomsbury Way,
London WC1A 2SG

An Albion Book

Conceived, designed and produced by
The Albion Press Limited
P.O. Box 52, Princes Risborough, Aylesbury, Bucks HP17 9PR

*Designer:* Emma Bradford
*Copy-editor:* Robyn Marsack
*Project Co-ordinator:* Elizabeth Wilkes

Reprinted by arrangement with Oxford University Press
Text copyright © Oxford University Press (i) 1934 (ii) 1936 (iii) 1937
Volume copyright © The Albion Press Limited 1990

ISBN 0 283 06000 X

**The illustrations are reproduced courtesy of:**

Ashmolean Museum, Oxford 11; Bridgeman Art Library (Bradford City Art Gallery and
Museums) 6, (Connaught Brown, London) 222, (Forbes Magazine Collection,
New York) 163, (Gavin Graham Gallery, London) 95, (Guildhall Art Gallery, London) 186,
194-195, (Louvre, Paris) 18, 111, (Musée D'Orsay, Paris) 103, (Museum of London) 35,
(Oldham Art Gallery, Lancs.) 2, (Phillips, The International Fine Art Auctioneers) 86,
(Private) 42, 54, 150, (Private, Paris) 98, (Roy Miles Fine Paintings, London) 138,
(Wolverhampton Art Gallery) 115, 174; Chris Beetles Ltd, St James's, London 50, 90-91, 158; Courtauld
Institute Galleries, London (Courtauld Collection) 214-215; Fine Art Photographic Library Limited 22, 27,
70, 74-75, 126, 130-131, 135; Mary Evans Picture Library 15; Copyright © 1989 by the
Metropolitan Museum of Art, New York, George A Hearn Fund, 1924 178; © Copyright The Museum of London
38-39, 47, 107, 199; the Trustees, The National Gallery, London 66; The Saint Louis
Art Museum 190; The Tate Gallery, London 210 (© 1978 Estate of Duncan Grant). All other pictures are from
private collections.

The publishers would like to thank the staff of all the organisations
listed above for their help, and also Danièle Kernec for her
assistance with picture research. Every effort has been made to
trace copyright owners, and the publishers apologize for any
inadvertent breach of copyright.

Typesetting and colour origination by York House, London
Printed and bound by Printer Industria Grafica S.A., Barcelona, Spain

# CONTENTS

*The Front Door, by Mary Elwell*

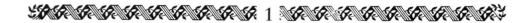

# 1

# 'A STAR DANCED'

A GIRL with four brothers older than herself is born under a lucky star. To be brought up in London, in the eighteen-seventies, by parents who knew how to laugh at both jokes and disasters, was to be under the influence of Jupiter himself.

This fell to my lot. My early memories run from 1870, when we moved into a big house in Canonbury, until 1879, when my happy childhood was abruptly ended. I hope to show that Victorian children did not have such a dull time as is usually supposed.

It is true that we had few toys, few magazines, few outside entertainments, and few means of getting about. But we got so much out of the few we had, by anticipation, by 'saving up', by exhaustive observation of the shop windows, and by the utmost use of the things we did achieve, that the well-to-do child of today can never get the same kind of pleasure. The modern ready-made well-stocked farm-yard, stable, or railway station, after a few days' admiration, asks for nothing but destruction, for there is nothing else to do about it.

For us, a large box of plain bricks was the foundation of all our doings. It served for railway stations, docks, forts, towers, and every kind of house. Another box of bricks, thin and flat with dove-tailed edges, enabled us to build long walls around our cities. Some two dozen soldiers, red for English and blue for French, mostly wounded and disarmed, carried out grand manoeuvres on specimens of granite and quartz arranged on the mantelpiece, and were easily mobilized anywhere. A packing-case did for a shop, where goods of all kinds were sold for marbles or shells or foreign stamps. The whole room was occasionally the sea, where a chair turned upside down was the *Great Eastern*, well and truly launched on the floor, for laying the Atlantic cable. A fat Lemprière's *Dictionary* did for a quay or a transport wagon or an enemy town.

We had several remains of ninepins, and plenty of marbles. I loved the colours of the marbles and furtively collected them. Their relative merits I knew, and how to prize a 'blood alley'; but learn to play I never could, preferring to flick or throw the marble, instead of using the thumb in the

masterly way that the boys insisted on.

A new toy was an event. Each one of our well-worn treasures must have made a sensation when it first arrived. One such event is graven on my memory. It was my fifth birthday, and I got up early and ran into my parents' room to be greeted. Laid out on the floor was a large and resplendent horse and cart. The horse was dapple-grey, all prancing and eyeing me in a friendly, willing way. The bright yellow cart, whose new stickiness I can still feel, had a movable back-piece that you could do something with. It would 'take off', and if you moved a wooden pin the cart tipped up; then you said 'gee-up' to the horse and all the goods would fall out. I had seen it done in the street, and promised myself no end of pleasure carting bricks for the boys.

Whether by design or not, we were allowed almost unlimited freedom, to imperil our lives without any sense of fear, and to invent our own amusements. We never had a nurse, or a nursery, or any one to supervise us. Instead of this we were given a room to ourselves – *all* to ourselves. In this matter we were better off than any other children we knew then or have known since. For our parents did the thing thoroughly. They provided a large table, a warm carpet, a fire whenever we liked, a large ottoman for storage and to serve as a window-seat; and left everything else to us. We chose the wallpaper and put what pictures we liked on the walls.

This room, which became a happy memory for us all through our lives, was called the 'study' – perhaps as a hint of its intention. The name added to its dignity without putting, as far as we were concerned, any notion of work into it. As time went on we did our home lessons in it, but the word 'study' is always associated in my mind with sheer fun.

So greatly was our possession of the study respected that I cannot remember my father or mother ever being in it, except on the occasions when they sat in the stalls during one of our theatrical displays, paying heavily for the privilege and for the programmes.

In one recess of the study there were four shelves, and by common consent each boy had one to himself. On his shelf he displayed his treasures. I remember the awe with which I gazed at my second brother's box of mathematical instruments, with bright compasses fitted into blue velvet grooves, and an ivory ruler that shifted into two for some strange purpose. He also had a big magnifying glass, which I always imagined had to be used when one 'magnified the Lord' in church. Some geological specimens were also displayed, but seemed to me of no use except for building forts.

My third brother, Charles, had quite other tastes. He was all for colour and variety, and one never knew what he would do next. At one time he had a rage for churches, and used to visit all the places of worship in the neighbourhood to see what they did. Then he arranged a cross and candles and flowers on his shelf, and got bits of coloured silk from Mother to make the correct liturgical changes, and I thus early learnt to expect purple in Lent, green for Trinity, and so on, and was able to impress many an elder who had 'really never noticed'

However, the main attraction for us all was the window. Our house stood at the corner of two roads, and our window had a good view down most of the length of one of them – Grange Road, affording us plenty of information of the doings of our neighbours and any passers-by. Up and down there went, much oftener than today, the hawkers of various goods, each with an appropriate cry: 'Flowers all a-blowing and a-growing', 'Ornaments for your fire-stove' (unbelievably hideous streamers of coloured paper), 'A pair of fine soles', bird-cages, iron-holders, brooms, brushes, and baskets. The long, wailing cry was a signal for us to crowd on to the ottoman to watch. Seeing our faces, the hawker would stop, look up eagerly, and hold up his goods. Several times we sent one round to the back-door with the encouraging words 'Mamma would like some.' Then we went to the top of the stairs to listen to the drama below: the hawker telling the housemaid that the Missus said she wanted a bird-cage, pause for journey of inquiry to the Missus, indignant denials, the return, abusive language from the hawker, a slammed door, glee in the study.

My second brother, who liked to talk about 'science', brought out the idea one day that a stone, if you wrapped it in a cloth, wouldn't break glass. We dared him to try it on the window. He said, oh yes, but perhaps it would be better to make it go some distance. We then suggested his trying it on the next-door-but-one's conservatory. I ran down to fetch a stone from the garden, and this was duly tied up in his handkerchief. He had been dared, and from a 'dare' there was no retreat. Whizz it went – crash through the glass roof. At this with one accord we became absorbed in pursuits of a studious nature, and after a bit began to feel that the affair had blown over. But then came a message by the housemaid that Master Vivian was wanted in the dining-room. There sat a frail old lady with Mother, who was holding the stone-laden handkerchief, marked with Vivian's full name. Mother was breathing out the direst punishments on him, but the injured one was pleading that she only wanted it not to happen again, and it didn't matter at all, that boys would be boys, bless them, she only wished she had a child of her own, and so on, until poor old Vivian was a mush of contrition.

In one of our amusements we were far ahead of the children of the time. My

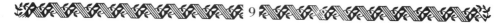

mother had a hobby, amounting to a passion, for water-colour painting, and she encouraged us in every way to draw and paint. She herself had a very large box of colours, and she gave me a little one made of wood, and a bigger, black-metal one to Charles, who could soon draw and paint far better than she could. She besought us at frequent intervals not to suck the brush. But you could never get a good point without sucking a bit, and since Mother laid so much stress on the evil effects of green (instant death apparently in some cases), we came to think that the other colours were not so bad.

We were rich too in another way, richer, so far as I can observe, than the average children of today. Our parents had accumulated a large number of books, which we were allowed to browse in as much as we liked. Scott, Dickens, Thackeray, Lamb, George Eliot, Tennyson, Byron, Coleridge, Disraeli, these were not 'taught' at school, or set as holiday tasks, but became part of our lives. The elder ones discussed them at table, and quoted from them, till the Micawbers and Becky Sharp and Lamb appeared to my childish mind as some former friends of Mother's, whom I recognized with delight later on when I read the books for myself. Rawdon was my eldest brother's favourite, and I knew 'same which I shot Captain Marker' long before I had the faintest notion of its meaning.

Occasionally the discussions became acrimonious. My eldest brother was one day making disparaging remarks about Tennyson, and my mother, all agitated in defence of her idol, fetched his poems from the shelf, and with a 'Listen now, children' began to declaim *Locksley Hall*. When she reached 'I to herd with narrow foreheads' she burst out, flinging down the book, 'What awful rubbish this is!'

That was one of the jolly points about Mother – she never minded saying what a fool she had been, was always proud to learn anything from the boys, and never gave us the 'Grown-up people know best' reproof.

I suppose there was a fear on my mother's part that I should be spoilt, for I was two years younger than the youngest boy. To prevent this danger she proclaimed the rule 'Boys first'. I came last in all distribution of food at table, treats of sweets, and so on. I was expected to wait on the boys, run messages, fetch things left upstairs, and never grumble, let alone refuse. All this I thoroughly enjoyed, because I loved running about, and would often dash up and down stairs just to let off my spirits. Of course Mother came in for some severe criticism from relations in this matter, but I have never ceased to thank her for this bit of early training.

The boys never failed to smile their thanks, call me 'good girl', do anything

*Bath Road, London, by Camille Pissarro*

for me that wanted a strong thumb or a long arm, and to bring me home something when they had been out and I was left at home. At one time, for instance, I collected threepenny bits, and Charles walked home one day rather than spend this, his last coin, on a tram, so that he might bring it to me.

I have never been able to decide which brother I liked best, for each had some special attraction for me. All four were absurdly unlike in character and appearance, and yet so close in age and size that no stranger could pick out the eldest.

First came Tom. His name was not short for anything, although his school authorities, in inscribing a prize, tried to dignify it in Latin by rendering the dative 'Tomato', providing us with a nickname for him at once. Tom always took my part through thick and thin, and would take me into partnership when I lost heavily at vingt-et-un. He told me that he had kissed my head when I was only one night old. I found it hard to believe that I had ever been so young. 'You couldn't walk or talk then,' he would say, 'you couldn't even sit up.' 'Oh, Tom,' I would protest, 'I *could* sit *up*!'

He used to take me on his knee and sing nursery rhymes or scraps from music-hall songs, jerking me up and down all the time. This he called doing the 'Jackley Troop', and I would clamour for it again and again.

My second brother had Mother's family name of Vivian. This I could not pronounce in my early days, and turned it into Dymond, which soon became Dym. He was the only one who took kindly to school-work, and devoted himself to mathematics. Reserved almost to being morose at times, he was a bit lonely, and was glad to have me as a confidante. He had a secret love of poetry,

*Tom in 1870*

*Dym in 1865*

and would get me up into the study alone and read aloud to me. He had a marvellously modulated voice, now tender, now thunderous. As I sat on the floor in open-mouthed admiration, he let himself go, moving me to pity over Sir Federigo's falcon, and to great excitement over the poor jester who cried out, 'I am, I *am* the King!'

Sometimes, too, he would show me a real scientific experiment. One day he said, 'Molly, would you like to see me turn water into wine, like it is in the Bible?' And he held up two wine-glasses full of water. 'Now watch,' he said, as he poured both into a bigger glass. And actually as I looked the water turned into claret. After this I was ready to believe almost anything. But one day he tried my credulity too hard. With quite a straight face he told me that the Earth was always moving. If it had been one of the other boys, I should have enjoyed the joke, and turned it off with an easy laugh, for they were always taking me in over something. But I didn't expect this from Dym, and his absurdity annoyed me. I can see myself now, in a starched pink frock sticking out all round, and a fat little bare leg with a white sock and shiny black shoe, stamping firmly on the floor and insisting, 'It doesn't, it doesn't!' – as solid in my own conviction as ever Galileo was in his. *Eppur NON si muove* was *my* mental reservation.

My third brother, Charles, was the only clever one among us. He worked hard at music and painting, but at nothing else would he do a stroke that could

*Charles in 1865*

*Barnholt in 1872*

be avoided. He was clever enough to make the tiniest bit of information do the work of volumes. He would find some remote fact about Zenobia or Savonarola, or some one like that, and then pretend to be shocked at the ignorance of those around him. Of course the family knew him, but his trick carried him far with outsiders. He was known to boast that he had never failed in an examination, while the family knew that he had never been in for one. In our continual arguments Charles always seemed to come out top, and his criticisms were merciless. As for me, I was snubbed continually, especially if I fished for a compliment or showed any symptom of self-pity. If I appeared in a new hat (very rare) Charles would exclaim, 'Well! of all the . . . ' He often told me how plain I was, and prophesied that I would grow fat like Aunt Polly. But there was rich compensation for all this in the things he would draw for me, the tunes he would play for me to dance, and the long exotic stories he would tell me, in the style of the Arabian Nights, making them up as he went along. And he was kind in unexpected ways, and when people weren't looking.

Nearest in age to me came Barnholt, and nearest in ideas and pleasant childishness. He had a sneaking interest in my dolls and foolish fancies. Lessons of all kinds were a never-ending burden to him. While Tom was good at Latin, Dym at mathematics, and Charles at music and drawing, poor old Barnholt shone in no direction. He would get me to hear him his 'po'try' and what he called 'me drivtivs' − lists of words to be learnt by heart, all derived from some Latin root. The only poem I can recall is Wordsworth's 'Pet Lamb'. What anguish it cost him to get it right! I don't think he ever got beyond the first verse. What insane master could set such a poem to healthy boys? The others used to tease him about it at meal-times, with invitations to 'Drink, pretty creature, drink'. Chaff, of course, Barnholt enjoyed, as one of the alleviations of home life, but detentions at school − they were the curse.

While anything smelling of school-work was poison to Barnholt, any little job of practical work, any errand, any risky adventure proposed, and he was on the spot. 'I say, Barney, do rope this box for me.' 'You might run and fetch me some stamps.' 'Look here, Barney, *you* go first.' There was no record of a refusal.

For some reason, different in each case perhaps, Barnholt was every one's favourite. In a moment of confidence Dym told me how, long ago, the family had gone for a holiday, leaving Barnholt, a tiny boy, with the servants (for some unknown reason). 'We came back unexpectedly', said Dym, 'and I ran ahead and caught sight of Barney in the window.' Here Dym shuddered as he added, 'His face was such a picture of misery that I have never been able to forget it.'

One reason, common to us all, for loving Barnholt a bit extra came from an incident of his fifth year. Although it happened when I was too young to know anything about it, I heard the story often enough to make the details always clear to me, even to the name of the culprit. This was a girl, Emma Lazelle, who took the four boys out for a walk one afternoon. I should have been taken too, no doubt, only that perambulators were newfangled things in those days, and we never had one; a baby too big to be carried stayed at home. In due course the party returned to tea, and only then discovered that Barnholt was missing.

'Where did you see him last?' 'Who was he walking with?' 'Where did you

*An Outing*

go?' 'Why didn't you keep looking round?' Mother rained such questions on Emma's head, without waiting for replies. But when she caught the word 'canal', and realized that Barnholt might have fallen into it, she stopped talking and faced despair. Fortunately my father came home soon, and went at once to the Police Station, assuring Mother that the canal was out of the question. He did not elaborate his reasons for this statement, but it acted well.

He drew blank at the Police Station, but was told that inquiries would be made.

Mother belonged to that school of thought that hopes to hasten a person's return by watching the road. For three nights and the best part of three days she hardly left the dining-room window which commanded the front gate. Strange to say, even the neighbours whose names we didn't know were interested. The wives saw Mother hour after hour in the window, and the husbands talked it over with my father in the train going to the City. It was this kind of primitive S.O.S. that was successful at last, for the police in those days had no efficient means of rapid communication.

On the afternoon of the third day, when Mother had begun to lose heart and strength, the gate was pushed open, and a neighbour from the house opposite ran up our path waving her hand excitedly. Mother rushed to the door and heard the words blurted out, 'Your little boy is found.' The watch at the

*No. 1 Canonbury Park North*

window was now a different business, and presently a policeman appeared leading Barnholt by the hand. The little fellow looked very jolly, and his first words were never forgotten: 'Are those for me?' – as he spied some ripe gooseberries on the table.

It seemed that he had wandered far afield, had been found by a policeman, and could give no information beyond that his name was Barney, his mother's name was Mamma, and he lived in the 'black house'. (This was because the next door to us had been newly painted, making ours look dirty.) The police had evidently been kind to him, but all that he was ever able to tell us was that they had given him some bread and butter and a halfpenny. In fact to him the incident had been a pleasant interlude.

As for me, the last of the family, my luck began at birth. Mother often told me of the scene. The doctor said to her, 'I think you have four boys, Mrs Thomas?' 'Yes, yes . . . and I suppose this is another,' she replied in a resigned

*Going to Bed, by E. K. Johnson*

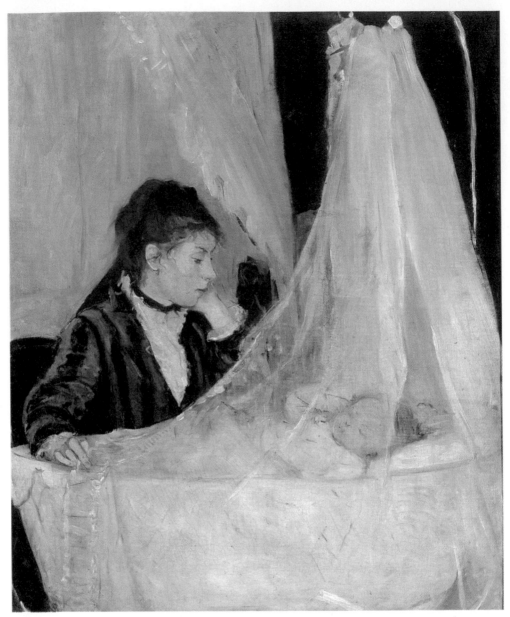

*The Cradle, by Berthe Morisot*

tone. 'Well, this is a little girl.' Whereupon my mother jumped up excitedly, crying, 'Let me see her, let me see her!' And it was only by swift appliances on the doctor's part that her life was saved. So from the very first I have never had the feeling of being an 'unwanted female'.

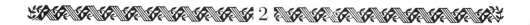 

# 2

# UPS AND DOWNS

A SETTLED income has its attractions possibly, but it can never be the fun of an unsettled one. My father was on the Stock Exchange, and wavered between great affluence and extreme poverty. Neither he nor Mother had a saving or economical disposition, but lived happily always, neither elated by wealth nor depressed by the lack of it.

We children were never aware of any money troubles, if such they could be called, for they made little difference to us. At no time were we allowed to spread our butter too thick. If things were going well, my father had no thought of enlarging his establishment or otherwise incurring bothers. His idea was that we should all enjoy ourselves a bit more along the old lines. When a shrinkage came we didn't notice much deprivation, or if we did it was put down to the weather. An oft-repeated family slogan was, 'Blessed is he that expecteth nothing, for he shall not be disappointed'. This happy-go-lucky attitude to life may be immoral from one point of view, but I have found it an excellent preparation for the continual uncertainties of my own lot.

An indulgence that Mother often permitted herself was a drive in Hyde Park. Not far from us was a 'Jobbing Stable', which provided us with a victoria and a sprucely dressed red-faced old coachman named Henry. He would dash up at 2 o'clock, flicking his whip, and Mother and I, all beautifully dressed, would get in, and be driven round among all the other carriages. How dull the saloon cars of today seem to me in comparison! Sometimes the Princess of Wales would pass us in the Row. I suppose I looked eager and excited and very young to be there, for once she smiled on me.

Now my father's pleasures took another direction. Not much more than a boy himself (for he married at the age of twenty-three) he loved cricket and all its social accompaniments. When money was plentiful he would take the boys, and often Mother and me as well, in a wagonette to a cricket match, and give us all a big lunch, and invite any cricketers home to supper. Mother had a kind of fixed idea of a spread at home, no matter where we had been, so that we were always glad to get back. I don't think she intended it exactly, but this certainty

*The London Stock Exchange, by Lockhart Bogle*

of a cheerful meal, even when it could not be expensive, on our return home had a subtle influence on us.

When there was no outing possible, we played cricket in our back garden, and broke windows frequently. Each smash was a joy to me, because I loved to watch the glazier at his miraculous job. He always gave me a lump of putty which I made into dolls' cups and saucers, and snakes for Barnholt.

Among the many cricketers coming and going there was one who was so constantly staying with us that I looked on him as a kind of uncle. But we always called him by his full name, Charlie Absalom, so that I thought it was one word. He was a well-known cricketer of the time, and played I think for England against Australia. His travelling-kit was extremely simple, and he used to say that his packing up was done in two movements – gathering up his night-shirt with one hand and aiming it into his portmanteau wherever that happened to be. His jolly face made up for the fierceness of his black beard, which I fancy he cultivated on the model of Grace.

Of course Charlie Absalom played cricket with the boys and me in the back garden, gave me underhands when he bowled and easy catches when he batted (not that I caught them), and broke his due share of windows. I can hear his cheery voice calling out, 'Coosh! there goes another!' Mother never scolded when anything whatever was broken. As she justly remarked, 'People don't break things on purpose, and if you blame them they get nervous, and are more likely to break more.' And she was far too sensible to suppose that you can play cricket properly with half your mind engaged in fearing what the ball may break.

Some of the highest spots of my childhood were those sunny Saturday afternoons when my father came home early with the word 'Kew' on his lips. Mother would throw aside any other plan, we all got ready in a trice, and trooped off in a body to the station at Canonbury. We did not make for the Gardens, as you might suppose, but always for the walk along the river bank to Richmond. This was wilder than the Gardens, allowing greater freedom of enterprise. Here were giant chestnut-trees, and competition in collecting the nuts. Whenever I pick up one today it brings back to me with its glossy lustre those rapturous afternoons. On our left we had glimpses of the Gardens, separated from us by a moat, and on our right ran the river, gay with rowing-boats, and every now and then sending ashore the wash of a pleasure-steamer, making 'real waves'.

After our walk, doubled by our scampering to and fro, we were ready for tea in a Richmond shop, and home again by train, to count our spoils and have endless games of conkers.

Another occasional playground for us was Epping Forest. The whole region was familiar ground to my father and mother, for here they had lived, during one of the depressed financial times, for several years in a tiny cottage, actually within the forest. It bore the charming name of Little Monkhams, and is now replaced by a row of villas. Little it certainly was, and I have often wondered how we all got in. Here the three youngest of us were born. Mother had a notion that it was improper to consult a doctor until the actual crisis, and Charles, who arrived unexpectedly at Christmas, was all but dead before the doctor could be fetched. The cottage was not only far from other habitations but was of the most primitive kind. Once, in a thunderstorm, the front windows blew out on to the lawn. Mother thought this very funny. But she must have been glad when a stroke of better fortune enabled us to move into the ample house in Canonbury.

*On the Thames, Barnes, by Atkinson Grimshaw*

I suppose it must have been during a lean year, when we were devoid even of servants, that my father would inaugurate some lark. One afternoon he came home early and suggested that it was just the sort of day for making toffee. The boys sprang to the idea, but Mother hesitated, as she didn't know quite how to make it. But when my father said that he knew all about it because they had made it at school once, we all followed him in a glad rush to the kitchen. Barnholt was sent to the grocer close by for 'a pound of his worst butter'. All grins, Barnholt flew forth on his errand. The grocer was annoyed at such a request, but, as Barnholt pointed out to him, if he had a best butter he must have a worst. Not seeing the obvious retort to this, he grumblingly served out a pound of something which my father declared to exceed his worst expectations. Meanwhile Mother had brought out sugar, and, after much searching of cupboards, some treacle. All was put in a saucepan and Dym was placed to stir it over the fire, while Charles measured out a tablespoonful of vinegar. My part was to get in every one's way and ask why each thing was done. My father's explanation of the vinegar was peculiar, having some strange reference to the Franco-Prussian War. When Mother had greased some flat tins the mixture was poured into them, and we had to wait a bit till it was set. I can't remember what it tasted like, but I know we were all in a glorious mess.

Another time it was a Welsh rabbit that my father had a mind for, and a syndicate was again formed for its creation. In this case the Franco-Prussian ingredient was a little beer. My father did the careful stirring this time, and two of the boys got round his legs making toast. Mother hovered around, shaking her head, prophesying indigestion and the doctor. But she ate her share and wished it had been bigger.

The best of these impromptu feasts was a positive shoal of sprats that my father came home with one evening. 'They're practically alive,' said he, 'and they were almost giving them away in Farringdon Market. Now, Mary, bring out your biggest frying-pan and some dripping, make up the fire, and you boys put the plates to warm. You shall have some fish on them before you know where you are.' And lo, it was so. There was a sizzling and a tossing, and soon the crisp little fish were tumbling on to our outstretched plates, while Mother was cutting bread and butter as fast as she could. I have had elegantly dressed sole at a grand dinner, salmon straight from the Dart, trout fresh from a Welsh stream, and perch that I caught myself in a Canadian river, but no fish has ever had the magic quality of those sprats 'given away' in London and cooked by my father.

*Fish Shop at Charing Cross, by Joseph Pennell*

# 3

# ROUND THE YEAR

**B**ANK holidays were much the same for Londoners as they are now — a day for remaining at home or for getting as far away as possible. In this matter we divided. Mother and I did the one, and my father and the boys the other. They used to start off by an early train, and take one of their colossal walks into the country, or else go fishing in the River Lea. Then off went the servants somewhere (probably to Hampstead Heath) for the entire day. Mother and I stayed at home to enjoy what she called 'the freedom of the wild ass', with no lessons, no proper meals, no duty walks, and above all no chance of callers. As soon as the boys had gone I used to watch for the big wagonettes full of children going off to Chingford or Epping for the day. They used to sing and wave flags, and I waved to them. After this the neighbourhood became sepulchral — 'silence like a poultice came to heal the blows of sound'. Mother must have been very clever in thinking up jolly things to do, for I can never remember feeling dull or out of it when the boys went off anywhere. She had the knack of vicarious enjoyment, and we used to live through what the others were probably doing: 'Now they are having their sandwiches', 'Now I expect they have caught some fish', 'Perhaps Charles has done a sketch'.

After tea it was my cue to watch at the window for the return of the wagonettes. I must say I took a grim pleasure in the peevish tones that came from the tired children, and the scoldings of the mothers, not to mention the lack of song and flag-waving. Our next business was to lay the cloth for supper and make a big spread for the hungry home-comers. At one such evening meal Mother exclaimed, 'How well you look, Dym!' The others smiled in a gratified way and spoke of the health-giving properties of country walking. It was not till many days had passed that they told her how Dym had fallen into the river and barely been saved from drowning. He had been taken to an inn, put into a hot bath, rubbed down, wrapped in blankets while his clothes were dried, and given whisky. No wonder, as he was hurried home as fast as possible, that he looked a bit rosy. He had a delicate chest, and had once been at death's door, while we crept about the house, alarmed at the arrival of a second doctor.

Strange as it seems today, when excursions are so cheap, a London family often went without any 'summer holiday' at all. There were certainly 'excursion trains', but they meant all that was horrible: long and unearthly hours, packed carriages, queer company, continual shuntings aside and waiting for regular trains to go by, and worst of all the contempt of decent travellers. We had a little rhyme about them which ended:

> *Grown old and rusted, the boiler busted*
> *And smashed the excursion train.*

So for a large family a trip to the sea-side was an expensive affair. In the years when we did not go to Cornwall, therefore we either bore the heat of London or had a fortnight at Walton-on-the-Naze. It looks very near on the map, but it was quite a business to get there. Liverpool Street was never the easiest of stations to start with, and then we had to change at Colchester. I can still see my mother's anguished face at this junction, as she got us all out, counted our many parcels, went to see if the heavy luggage had been shifted, made repeated inquiries (so as to make sure) as to the right platform, and then packed us all in again for the final lap. As a rule, my father could only get away for weekends, when he and Charlie Absalom or an uncle would come by steamer.

The cabman at Walton knew us, and the landlady at the lodgings welcomed us, and all the troubles of the journey were quickly forgotten as we rushed to greet the sea. Although the place has now been improved beyond recognition with hotels, restaurants, and new types of boarding-houses, the sea and its attractions are just the same. Buckets and spades are the same pattern and colour, sand-castles and fortifications no grander or stronger than ours, donkeys just as recalcitrant. Indeed, we had one advantage over the children of today, for no one had discovered that continual paddling was bad for you, so we were barefoot all the time, in and out of the water, scrambling over breakwaters, fishing for crabs, collecting shells and stones, and screwing our toes into the wriggly sand.

At an ill-starred moment Mother decided that I was old enough to bathe like the boys. She selected for her experiment a nice pool beside a long, low rock, discreetly far from the main beach. I was quite excited at the idea of doing something like the boys, consented to be stripped, and paddled boldly forward. Mother thought that all she need do was to carry on with her sewing, and throw me words of encouragement. 'Sit down, darling. Splash about a little. Go a little farther in. Don't mind getting wet all over. It won't hurt you. . . .' But there I stood, not quite knee-deep, fixed, with a safety-first idea. Now Mother had no use for obstinacy, and thinking me no more than obstinate she laid aside her sewing with some sharpness, walked along the rock, stooped and seized my readily outstretched hand, at the same time giving me a little jerk forward and downward into the water. Aware now that my last moments were approaching, I pulled my hardest, Mother's foot slipped, and flop! she went headlong into the pool. Her summer frock, a mass of flounces and ribbons, her beautiful wide hat . . . they hardly bear thinking about. She managed to dress me somehow, to gather up her sewing, and walk back to our lodgings, dripping water all the way, adding greatly to the cheerfulness of the 'front'.

When my father was told of it he said I ought to be punished, 'because a child should be taught to recognize a disaster when it happens'. However, he added, 'You punish her, dear. It will come better from you.' As this was his well-known method of getting out of something he hated doing, they both laughed. The only upshot was that Mother was promised a new dress, I had a big hug from my father on the quiet, and my bathing lessons were postponed.

To vary our shore pleasures we used to strike inland, and were in real country at once, for there were no 'respectable' roads and villas surrounding the place. Frinton lane was a lonely walk, almost alarmingly so, with its trees overhead. To me it was the 'shady lane', down which Tom and Jane met their death in the poem from eating 'scarlet berries'. Mother's horror of deadly nightshade was only equalled by her fear of green paint. The mushrooms and blackberries we brought in added pleasantly to our landlady's limited cuisine. Her apple tarts and puddings were really clove confections flavoured with apple.

When the boys were off on some long wet-weather tramp, Mother and I stayed in our lodgings. She would sketch something from the window, or else do a bit of necessary sewing. She hated sewing so much that she generally stood to do it. I have inherited both the hatred and the posture, but am still puzzled at the reason for standing. Does it get it over sooner? At home, Mother coped in a simple way with the eternal mending required for the family. She hired an extremely old maid to spend every Friday with us. There she sat all day, at a little table in the kitchen window, mending. She would never lend her scissors, not for a moment, and if I asked her to 'button me up' she would do it very slowly, and say, 'Patience is a virtue.' This sounded like a text, but I believe it was a hideous thought entirely her own.

*Wool-winding, by George Goodwin Kilburne*

While the boys were off, and Mother busy, I was completely happy with a wooden stool on four legs, padded with red velvet. It was a treasure belonging to the landlady, who brought it out for me specially, with the request that the young gentlemen should not sit on it. Mother, knowing the young gentlemen, hid it always until they were out of the way, and then I had such glory with it

*The Lord Mayor's Procession*

that it compensated for my being left at home. It became in turn a table, a bed, a funeral coach, a train, a station, a pirate vessel for stealing Mother's brushes or cotton, and oftenest of all it was Bucephalus, on which I careered about the room, conquering country after country. The boys returned all too soon.

Back again in London we had to settle down to a long stretch of 'everyday-ness'. October is bound to be enjoyable always, but November meant fogs, trees bared before they had time to get red and gold, and perhaps 'doing without a fire' because it was not quite cold enough. The one excitement to be certain of was the Lord Mayor's Show, coinciding with the Prince of Wales's birthday, and a school holiday. Needless to say, I never saw the Show myself. The boys always went, and came home full of their struggles with the crowd and their prowess in elbowing their way to the front. It seemed to me something like the way Cinderella went to the ball, from their description of the coach. They always brought home for me a little book, that opened out to nearly a yard of coloured pictures, displaying all the features of the Show. This was called 'A Penny Panorama of the Lord Mayor's Show', and the name pleased me so much that for days afterwards I would go about the house pretending to be a hawker, crying:

> *Buy my Panorama, my penny Panorama,*
> *My penny Panorama of the Lord Mayor's Show.*

Mere river-side excursions were indulged in at any time, the steamer trip to Greenwich and back being the usual one. For the boys, of course, not me. All I culled from them was a new chant for my play: 'Ease her, back her, stop her', and the longer instructions: 'When in danger with no room to turn, ease her, stop her, go astern', and 'When you see three lights ahead, port your helm and show your red'.

Nowadays it is difficult to realize that no Christmas preparations were made until the week before the day itself. All our excitement was packed into a short space. The boys were on holiday, and all over the place. Mother was mostly in the kitchen, presiding over mincemeat and puddings. I was set to clean currants, squeeze lemons, and cut up candied peel. Barnholt lent a hand at chopping the suet, but kept making raids on the lumps of suger tucked away in the candied peel, which he assured me were very hard and nasty in the mincemeat, but had no ill effects on him.

Tom and Dym kept going to Upper Street to get stationery, cards, and presents from the shops. Charles spent his time in painting home-made Christmas cards. Midday dinner was a noisy buzz of comparing notes on the morning's doings, and having a look at what Charles had produced. The afternoons were generally given up to the preparation of our annual play. It fell to Tom to devise the plot, and to Charles, the Bully Bottom of the family, fell nearly everything else. He took the part of the villain or the comic washer-woman, and kept thinking up ideas for improving the parts of the others. He taught me how to act when I wasn't speaking, how to listen with agitation, how to do 'by-play', how to swoon, and once even how to die. Dym was usually the hero, a bit stiff, but always dignified. Barnholt had to be given a part with little to say, because, however willing, he could not be relied on to remember the words, or improvise other ones. He would be a coachman or a footman, or perhaps only the scene-shifter. What he really loved was to be the policeman, coming in at the crisis with a ''Ere, what's all this?', pulling out his note-book, wetting his thumb, and taking people's addresses. He knew his stuff for this perfectly, but it wouldn't always fit into melodrama.

Tom, to my great comfort, was prompter, and saved me from many a breakdown when I was swamped with nervousness. I didn't actually forget my

*Stirring the Christmas Pudding*

words, but I should have done if Tom hadn't stood by smiling at me behind the screen.

Christmas Eve was the day we liked best. The morning was a frenzied rush for last rehearsals, last posting of cards, last buying of presents. My father came home early, laden with parcels. The tea-table was resplendent with bon-bons (crackers), sweets, and surprise cakes with icing on the top and three-penny-bits inside. The usual 'bread and butter first' rule was set aside, and we all ate and talked and laughed to our heart's content.

Then followed the solemn ascent to the study for the play. The boys had borrowed chairs from the bedrooms, and placed them in two rows: the front (stalls) for Father, Mother, and any aunt, uncle, or visitor who happened to be there, and the back (pit) for the servants, who attended with much gigglement.

Personally I was thankful when this nerve-strain was over, and we all crowded down into the breakfast-parlour. Here, earlier in the day, Mother and I had arranged the presents — a little pile for each, and we all fell upon them with delight. We were never fussed up with a Christmas tree or stockings or make-believe about Santa Claus. Perhaps we were too hard-headed. Perhaps Mother considered that waking up in the small hours to look at stockings was a bad beginning for an exciting day. As it was, we had nice time before bed for peeping into our new books, and gloating over all the fresh treasures.

Christmas Day itself followed a regular ritual. Service at St Paul's was exactly the same as it is now, the same hymns and even the same decorations (knots of red velvet hung on the pillars). The post was the next excitement, and we displayed our cards on the mantelpiece. The traditional dinner of turkey and plum pudding and dessert was followed by a comatose afternoon, during which Barnholt cooked chestnuts incessantly on the bars of the grate, tossing them to us as they were done.

The evening festivities began with the ceremony of punch-making. This was always my father's special job, and he spread himself over it royally. Quanti-ties of loaf sugar and lemons were assembled, and a very large glass jug. A kettle of water was on the fire. The lemon-juice and sugar were stirred together at the bottom of the jug, then a tumblerful each of rum and brandy were added. Carefully my father then filled the jug with boiling water. Carefully, because once the boiling water smashed the jug, and everything splashed over the dining-room table. He laughed and called for all the ingredients over again. 'We've lost the punch,' said he, 'we needn't also lose a bit of our lives by crying over it.'

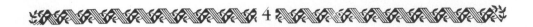 

# 4

# SAILING NEAR THE WIND

NOTHING peculia (sic) happened today.' Such is the entry again and again in my first diary, a large 'Renshaw' for 1876, presented by my father, filled in with anxious care, and preserved even till today. The main 'care' was that events being so few I was driven to record even the fact of going to bed. My outside amusements were mainly pale reflections of what the boys told me about theirs. The Agricultural Hall was within easy reach of us, and I wondered what the boys found so attractive in a place with such a name. Of course I was never allowed to go there myself, but gathered that it was not all concerned with farming and cattle and pigs. At one time a man named Weston used to walk round and round the Hall to see how long he could keep it up. This seemed to me a foolish game, but the boys liked to watch him, especially when he had ten minutes' rest, and fell asleep in the arms of his attendants.

Far more exciting to me were the accounts the boys brought home from the Polytechnic. The name had a gayer sound, and here there was a Diving-Bell. You went into a little room inside a big bell, and were let down into water. So they said, but of course I didn't believe it. However, it sounded a delightful take-in, and I used to shout about the house, 'This way for the Diving-Bell.' Dym took the trouble to show me, with the aid of a tumbler, a rag, and a pail of water, how the diving-bell worked. I was amazed, but still unbelieving that people would trust themselves to go under water just because a rag in a tumbler managed to somehow to keep dry.

Strange as it seems I was never taken to anything more exciting than a picture gallery, not even to a pantomime at Christmas. Not even to the Tower or the Crystal Palace or Madame Tussaud's — places to which the boys had to conduct country cousins, with profuse grumblings. I suppose it was their expressed boredom with such excursions that reconciled me to staying at home. However, whenever there was any game afoot actually in the house or garden I was allowed to join in. Some of these were kept secret, lest they should be labelled 'naughty', but I cannot remember that we were ever punished severely. An occasional putting in the corner for me, and a threatened 'slippering' of the boys by my father if they were too noisy – these were the usual penalties. When one of the boys had really annoyed Mother, she would address him as 'Sir', and send him to have his hair cut. This does not sound so bad as it in fact was. Our only available hairdresser had a strange habit of keeping a customer waiting for a half to three-quarters of an hour. There was nothing to do but stare at a fern and a picture of Cromwell sitting at his daughter's death-bed.

A kind of family 'common law', an unwritten code, seemed to have existed from the beginning of time and was accepted as inevitable by us all. One rule was that one went to bed the moment the word was said, without argument or plea. Another was that one ate up everything on one's plate. Tom once had to finish the mustard which he had too liberally taken, and I can still recall the swelling in my throat as I bolted my last piece of blancmange. Another law was that we must never be rude to servants. Beyond these there was nothing criminal, except perhaps taking Mother's scissors for our private ends.

So infrequent were my own punishments that I recall vividly the two occasions when I deserved them and obtained them. One morning I was bored with my lessons, looked round for some little drama, and proclaimed myself thirsty. Already I suppose I had discovered that a mother can require resistance to hunger, but not to thirst. 'Run downstairs then, dear, and ask cook to give you a glass of water.' Down I went, and after a decent delay returned with the report that cook had refused to give it to me. Now, thought I, for some fireworks. Alas! Mother didn't even send for the cook or institute inquiries, or appear disturbed at all. She said, 'Write in your diary, "I told a lie today".' There was no escaping it, my beautiful diary had to be thus disfigured, staring at me. And to this day I think the punishment was excessive.

The other disgrace was still more memorable because it was a strain, and the only one, between me and my father. Charles was reading Hans Andersen: I wanted the book, asked for it, fussed for it, and finally broke into tears. This brought my father into the room, and I hoped for the best. But he became dreadfully serious, led me upstairs, and administered a whipping. Then he explained that it is as bad for a girl to cry for what she wants as for a boy to plant a blow. I might cry a very little if I was badly hurt, but never, never must I cry just to get something.

Adventures of a kind that were not forbidden mainly because Mother didn't know about them were plentiful enough, and usually carried out in the back garden. One boy would dare another to some perilous act, while I was a delighted looker-on, half dreading and half hoping for the worst. An acacia-tree stood at the end of the garden. Into this the boys would climb and then swing themselves over into the street – a considerable drop. Another feat was to walk along the top of the high, narrow wall, endowed with bits of glass. The most dangerous of all was climbing round a ledge, some two inches wide, that ran along the house over the area. The boy who attempted this had to flatten himself, spread out his arms, and press his palms against the wall. This particular part of the back premises was invisible from any window, and was therefore chosen when we were 'sailing near the wind', as my father called any near approach to the sinful.

I was merely an onlooker, but was allowed on one occasion to join in an open-air smoking concert in these back premises. Barnholt had been sent out to buy some 'jumbles' – a thin kind of gingerbread about the size of a saucer, so crisp that it curled up. I was given a jumble, a front seat, and (bliss beyond words!) a pipe to put in my mouth. All was in train when who should casually open the back door but Mother . . . I remember that my jumble fell in fragments at my feet and that the rest of the incident was a storm of scolding that I should dare to put a pipe in my mouth. The crime had only been omitted from the ten commandments because not even Moses could imagine that a little girl should so disgrace herself. And so on. It lasted a long time. But how I did regret not having had one bite of my jumble.

'How I wish I were a boy!' Mother caught me saying this aloud one day, and promptly told me that this was a wicked thought. She did not go on to give a reason, but merely insisted that it was splendid to be a girl, and with such exuberant enthusiasm that I was quite convinced. My father's slogan was that boys should go everywhere and know everything, and that a girl should stay at home and know nothing. Often the boys must have been sorry for me, and one day when I exclaimed, 'How lovely it must be to go on the top of a bus!', Dym first laughed at the idea, and then suddenly said, 'I say, Barney, let's take her.' Barnholt, of course, was only too ready, and I rushed to get my things on before something could happen to stop us. If I had been asked to a royal ball I couldn't have been more excited.

Inside a bus I had often been with Mother when we went to Shoolbred's or Peter Robinson's for a morning's shopping. The bus was a box lined with blue velvet, made to carry five each side, of whom Mother declared that the fattest always sat next her and half on her, for she was very small. No air got in, except when the door was opened, for the little windows admitted only some so-called light. Straw on the floor, designed to keep our feet warm, was apt to get very

*The Bayswater Omnibus, by George William Joy*

wet and dirty. When the bus started the door was firmly shut, the conductor remaining outside with no visible means of support. Presently he would let down the top of the door, put his head in, and ask, 'Any for the Angel?' – or whatever the next stage happened to be. Then fares were handed up to him (no tickets were used), and he made a mark with a stumpy pencil on a yellow sheet. I knew what this sheet was called, because all I could amuse myself with during the journey was to read the directions beseeching the passengers to see that their fares were 'duly registered on the waybill at the door'. We stopped anywhere, for plenty of passengers rather than rapid progress was the main idea. I reckon that the journey from Islington to the West End took a good deal over an hour. Wedged as we were, it was impossible to see anything out of the tiny windows, and the journey was sheer boredom. What with the lack of air, the jerks of the frequent stops, and the jolting over the stone-paved roads, I was usually too ill to stay the course, and we had to get out some distance before our required shop.

Mysterious as was the mode of attachment of the conductor, the means of getting on to the top was still more so. From the glimpses I had from inside people disappeared bit by bit, their boots last. Of course no woman ever went up. And now, here was I, going to do it myself!

I rushed up again to the study, all dressed, and Dym surveyed me and said I would do. My outdoor clothes in winter never varied: a hat of real sealskin that stood all weathers and could not wear out, neither could it blow off, for it was fastened round my chin by elastic; my warmth was secured by a 'cross-over' — a strip of tartan about two yards long that crossed over in front and fastened behind, leaving my arms free. The worst worry in going out were my boots, which came far above the ankle with endless buttons that needed a hook to do them up.

*Buses, by Joseph Pennell*

Dym decided that it would be best for us to walk to the little side street not far away, where the 'Favourite' buses began their journeys. Here we were able to make the ascent at leisure. Dym went up first, then hung down and pointed out the tiny ledges on which I had to put my feet, stretching out his hands to pull me up, while Barnholt fetched up the rear in case I slipped. On the top was what they called the knifeboard — a raised partition along the middle, with seats each side. How people stuck on to them I couldn't imagine. But the boys had better designs: they scrambled down on to the seat in front, by the driver, and got me there too. 'Come along, Missy,' said the driver, who was just

settling himself for his journey, and I was safely tucked in between him and Dym, with Barnholt on his other side.

How powerful the horse looked from this point of view, how jolly to hear the chuckings and whoas, and to see the whip flourished about, but only gently touching the horse. 'I never whips old Rosy,' the driver told me. 'She's been with me six years and knows what I want. I use the whip like chatting to her.' How pitiable were all the people on foot! How contemptible the passengers who went inside! Barnholt, as look-out man, kept calling my attention to things in the shops, and to people doing mysterious jobs in first-floor windows. One room was a nursery, where a boy was riding on a rocking-horse, and in one garden we passed there was a swing with a boy going very high.

We feared to go the whole length of our twopenny ride in case we should be late for tea, so we asked the driver to pull up for us. In my haste to show him how well I could get off by jumping down to Dym in front I fell right into the muddy street. But no harm was done, and the boys picked me up, and we ran home as fast as we could and slipped in at the back door. There was no hiding my mud, and 'Wherever have you been?' cried Mother. 'Oh, just for a run with the boys, and I fell.' This was true enough to pass my conscience. Dym was non-plussed, but Barnholt immediately took up the tale of a fine new shop where they sold cricket-bats and bags and things, and how he had thought it better not to spend the shilling Uncle Alfred had given him. On this wave of virtue my muddy dress was forgotten, and we went into tea with no further questions asked.

In some escapades I was actually useful. November 5th fell one year on a half-holiday. Tom was away at school, Dym was staying at school to play fives, Barnholt for once had no detention, so we three youngest were free for anything. Naturally Charles had an idea. 'Why not make a guy and go round the streets with it?' We could disguise ourselves so that nobody would know us . . . do let's.'

Barnholt then suggested that I could be the guy because I was so small. Indeed the boys often used to give me a chair-ride by clasping their own wrists for a seat while I steadied myself on it by putting my arms round their necks. But Charles had seen in the back kitchen an old cane chair without a back, and he thought this would be better. Mother was intending to pay some calls and was safely in her bedroom getting her things on. So we crept downstairs and told the servants what we wanted to do. These servants had been with us

*St Pancras Hotel and Station from Pentonville Road: Sunset, by John O'Connor*

simply for ever and joined in any of our larks with enthusiasm. A guy going by was exciting enough to them, but to dress one was a joyous break to a dull afternoon. They found the little chair, sat me in it, and draped the red cotton kitchen tablecloth round me. Meanwhile Barnholt had made paper cocked hats for us all and Charles provided us with black moustaches from the soot of a candle-flame. My plaid cross-over was pinned in a martial style over Barnholt's shoulder, and the housemaid lent Charles her black cape to make him look villainous. As I had my hands free the candle was put in one, and a tin box for contributions in the other. Charles wrote GUNPOWDER on a sheet of note-paper to place behind the tin. At last all was ready, and as soon as we heard Mother close the front door we stole out at the back, staggering up the area steps with difficulty.

Making as quickly as possible for a side street we certainly attracted little attention that would distress us, but neither did we attract the pennies. Charles saw that we needed to make some kind of *noise*, and he started a hymn. This sounded so absurd in the street that Barnholt and I shook with laughing in trying to say that earth hath many a noble city. Well, we knew that laughter would be no use – we must look pathetic if we wanted pennies. Just as we were beginning to feel rather damped we heard the dismal strains of an organ-grinder. 'The very thing!' cried Charles, and we wobbled off in the direction of the sound. I can see now the broad grin of the man as he readily consented to our going along with him. Soon another brain-wave came over Charles, and he asked the man to help carry the chair while he himself had a try at grinding the organ. Of course Barnholt wanted to try too, and the man said they might take it in turns.

Then indeed success began. 'Tommy make room for your uncle' had new interest. Jaded hearers were astonished to find the well-known air first rendered by Charles as a funeral march, and then by Barnholt as a mad gallop. Windows were thrown open, and amid cries of 'poor little souls' pennies and halfpennies came hurtling down. I was placed on the ground while the coins were gathered up, and my tin box began to fill. After some of this triumphant proceeding, the organ-grinder became aware that we had only gone through two streets. He said he must get along faster, as he had to do his 'round'. This was a new idea to me, that he had a round like a milkman. But when I came to think of it I remembered that on regular days and at regular hours an organ-grinder would be heard in our road. People looked to see him, he said, and it would never do to disappoint them.

We had some trouble to get him to take the box of money. 'No, take it home to your por ma,' said he, and we had to explain that it was only a lark, and that 'por ma' wouldn't like it at all. So we settled matters by taking a penny each, which we turned into acid drops at a little shop at the corner. Fortunately it was now getting dusk, and we hoped to slip home without being seen by any one who knew us. As luck would have it we came full tilt on Mother at the gate. She was so glad, however, to get home after a solid hour's calling ('aching behind the ears with being polite', as she described it) that she only laughed at our appearance and said, 'You naughty children, go and wash at once.' We were sensible enough not to mention the episode of the organ-grinder and the moneys received, let alone that the vicar had met us and dropped a whole sixpence into the box. We suspected that he recognized us, but he played the game and kept very grave.

*Molly in 1872*

*The Breakfast Table, by George Clausen*

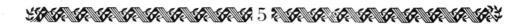 

# 5

# UP TO ELEVEN

I'm six years old this very day,
And I can write and read,
And not to have my own way
Is very hard indeed.

THE boys had the advantage of me in going about, but I had the advantage of them in not being sent to school. Until my eleventh year I was saved from the stupefying influence of such a place. Mother undertook all that she thought necessary for me, and was very liberal-minded about it. There was no nonsense about a time-table, but a good morning's work was carried out. Breakfast over, my father seen off to the City and the boys to school, Mother would 'go round the house'. This ritual involved such duties as putting out sheets, counting the wash, ordering the dinner, arranging which of the tradesmen was to be blamed for something.

Then Mother would summon me to her side and open an enormous Bible. It was invariably at the Old Testament, and I had to read aloud the strange doings of the Patriarchs. No comments were made, religious or otherwise, my questions were fobbed off by references to those 'old times' or to 'bad translations', and occasionally Mother's pencil, with which she guided me to the words, would travel rapidly over several verses, and I heard a muttered 'never mind about that'.

After the reading, every word of one verse had to be parsed. Very soon I learnt the queer power of the preposition, for in such a phrase as 'the word of the Lord' I was never allowed to say that 'Lord' was in the objective, because it involved adding that it was governed by the preposition 'of', and it was irreverent to say that the Lord was governed by anything at all. At the same time I knew that He *was* in the objective, and that 'of' had done it.

After this effort Mother usually gave herself up to her hobby of water-colour painting, seated at the end of the dining-room table, while I carried on by myself with a little reading, sewing, writing, or learning by heart, in the offing. Every now and again I would come to the surface with a question about the meaning of a word, or a bit of hemming that needed pressing down, or a piece of French poetry to be 'heard'. As for English poetry, it needed no hearing, because I declaimed it about the house, but the French had to be rendered carefully, with poise and a touch of éclat. I can still repeat 'Le rat de ville et le rat des champs' from the drilling of those early days.

My English history was derived from a little book in small print that dealt with the characters of the kings at some length. I learnt how one was ruthless alike to friend and foe, and how another was so weak that the sceptre fell from his nerveless grasp. I seemed to see it falling. The book had no doubts or evidence or sources, but gave all the proper anecdotes about cakes, the peaches and new ale, never smiling again, the turbulent priest, and the lighted candle. I am glad that I had these at the credulous stage, and in this unhesitating form. They were much more glowing than if they had been introduced by the chilling words 'it is said that'. I never read beyond Queen Elizabeth, and was really shocked when Mother told me one day that a king had his head cut off. I rained questions on her: Who did it? Why? What had he done? Why did they let them do it?

Not as a lesson, but for sheer pleasure, did I browse in *A Child's History of Rome*, a book full of good stories that spared none of the details about Regulus in the barrel, the death of Gracchus, Marius in the pond, and Sulla's cold-blooded slaughters.

The home boasted an enormous atlas almost as big as the hearthrug, that I could only cope with when it was laid out on the floor. From this I culled a good deal, but all I can recall of my little geography book is the opening sentence, 'The Earth is an oblate spheroid', and the statement that there are seven, or five, oceans. I never could remember which, but knew it was an odd number.

For scientific notions I had Dr Brewer's *Guide to Science*, in the form of a catechism. The author was a Trinity Hall man, who must have made a wide appeal, for my copy (dated 1869) is of the twenty-sixth edition. It opens firmly thus: '*Q*. What is heat?', and the *A*. comes pat: 'That which produces the sensation of warmth.' Later on, however, a modern note of doubt creeps in, for we get: 'What is light?' to which the *A*. is 'The *unknown* cause of visibility.' But the field of ignorance is very small. Some of the information is human and kindly. Thus we have: '*Q*. What should a fearful person do to be secure in a storm? *A*. Draw his bedstead into the middle of his room, commit himself to the care of God, and go to bed.' To this is added, in very small print, 'No great danger needs really to be apprehended.'

I spoke of sewing, but I never progressed beyond hemming. Endless pocket-handkerchiefs for the boys were cut from the parent roll of linen, turned down at the edges by Mother, and hemmed by my hot little hands while the linen was all stiff and shiny. Charles said that I put the needle in one day and took it out the next. But that was an exaggeration.

My dislike of sewing was as nothing compared to my hatred of sums. This was the correct word, for I never did anything but addition. Mother's arithmetic was at the level of the White Queen's, and I believe she was never quite sound about borrowing and paying back, especially if there were a nought or two in the top row. I had a slate on which Mother put long lists of figures to be added, enough to keep me quiet for a good long time. But as the sum had been made out of her head she had to check it by working it herself. Next to ready-made pocket-handkerchiefs I think the greatest boon of modern invention would have seemed to her an arithmetic book of easy sums with answers. We certainly possessed a badly printed, dilapidated old Colenso's *Arithmetic*. But this was vaguely connected in Mother's mind with some one who doubted the creation of the world, and not reliable, or at least not to be encouraged. Often when sums were adumbrated I felt a little headachy, and thought I could manage a little drawing and painting instead.

Obviously there was no hard-and-fast routine in my morning's work, and if the weather turned out tempting, Mother would dismiss all idea of lessons and take me out, either for a long walk, or into the West End for some shopping, or by train to Hampstead for a sketching expedition. Such times were the best part of my education, for Mother had had a richly varied and adventurous life. The darker parts of it I never knew till long afterwards, but her outlook on life, her opinions on people, and her matured wisdom became a part of me. On our long tramps together, in the intervals of my bowling my hoop, I would induce her to tell me stories. She had to rake her memory for tales from Shakespeare, Jane Austen, Scott, or any novel she had ever read. But what I liked best, and insisted on hearing again and again, was a description of her own doings when she was a girl. Her first school had been at Falmouth, and after that she had gone to a 'finishing' school at Bath.

This was in the reign of William IV, when Bath was the most fashionable pleasure resort of the day. The numbers in the school were limited to six, with as many teachers as pupils. Visiting masters attended for French, music, and philosophy. Mother was frequently given lessons alone. Manners were attended to with special care. When the young ladies were invited out to tea they were set down to a meal of thick bread and butter before starting, in order that their appetites should appear elegant. They were commanded to leave something on their plate, however pleasing the dish. Nevertheless the work in school must have been solid, for Mother could speak French fluently, had done a good deal of Latin, had staggered through Locke and Berkeley, and knew as much as could be expected about the movements of the moon and where to look for the various stars as the year went on.

By the way, Mother started me in Latin at a very tender age. I can remember dancing round a small table chanting ''mo, 'mas, 'mat, 'mamus, 'matis, 'mant'. My enthusiasm was rather dashed when Tom suggested that I ought to begin the Passive Voice. This seemed to me an unnecessary complication – soldiers could so easily *go* on to the wall, without being *sent* there.

In addition to Mother's stories of her school-days she used to describe her amusements in her Cornish home. She was a fine horsewoman, and had tales of giving the men 'a lead' over a high gate in the hunting-field. Balls were rare events, but they were full of go, and evidently not the stately and prim affairs of mid-Victorian times. The day following a ball was the best fun, for it was the practice of all the young men to go round on horseback and call on the girls, to 'ask how they were', and so on. Mother used to smile to herself as she dwelt on this pleasant habit.

Very few girls of her time had travelled as much as Mother. Hardly had she left school before she accompanied her father abroad on his mine-prospecting journeys. The most adventurous of these was a tour in Spain. Here the so-called roads were so bad that horseback was the only means of getting about. Mother was frequently in the saddle from early morning till sundown. I thought this was lovely, but she pointed out that one could have enough even of riding. Inns were of the most primitive. One large sleeping-apartment often had to do duty for all the guests. Early one morning, after a night of this kind, the innkeeper tiptoed softly into the room and besought them in whispers to leave quietly and as soon as possible. He told them that a number of *banditti* had got wind of there being rich English people in the place, and were intending to have their money or their lives. He had given them plenty of drink which they were now sleeping off, lying about the door. In a trice Mother was ready to start, for of course she had never undressed. True enough, there lay some fifteen of the fiercest-looking ruffians, each with a gleaming knife by his side, but fortunately all snoring. They had purposely disposed themselves so that no one could pass through the outer 'living-room' without treading on them. Mother gathered up her riding-skirt and stepped widely and swiftly, choosing when she could a spot near a knife, so that she could seize it if the man stirred. Rushing to the stable she saddled her horse – a job to which she

*New Oxford Street, by J. Absolon*

was well accustomed – and rode off, knowing that her father would manage better with her out of the way. He soon overtook her, having waited only to repay the sensible innkeeper.

An experience in Christiania was of a different and absurd nature. A visitor in the hotel was a famous chess-player, and was complaining in the lounge that he found it so difficult to get a good game – any one who would stand up to him. Whereupon it was suggested to him that Mother could play very well and would keep him busy. At this Mother was horrified, but instead of singing low she merely declined rather haughtily, for she thought the man odiously conceited. However, he so begged and implored, and Mother's friends so egged her on with 'Do beat him, Mary', in undertones, that she said, 'Very well, then, I will give you just one game, but no more.' Overjoyed, he hurried out the pieces, they sat down, and the friends watched eagerly. Mother fool's-mated him. It was one of those moments that make life worth living. She rose, bowed, and retired from the scene, leaving him a lather of excuses and annoyance – a humbler man.

Such reminiscences were for country walks. A visit to the West End was a different affair. My delight was to walk down Regent Street and gaze in the shop-windows, pointing out all the things I would like to have. And this was as good a piece of education as any other, for I early acquired the Londoner's ability to enjoy things without buying them. For even in our palmiest days Mother never dreamt of buying anything she didn't really want. But how we both gazed at and admired exotic fruits, exquisite note-paper, china jugs (a weakness of Mother's), and especially drawing-materials with serried rows of paints. One day in Bond Street Mother noticed a sailor hat, poised alone in a window. 'How nice and simple! the very thing for you!' she exclaimed, and went in to ask the price. 'Three guineas, Madam.' She nearly fell out of the shop.

A picture gallery was often a reason for our going into the West End. The Turner room at the National was as familiar to me as the dining-room at home, and Mother early taught me to regard these pictures as my own property. 'Given to the nation,' she would roll on her tongue as she feasted her eyes on the *Fighting Téméraire*. Then there were the Dudley and the Grosvenor galleries, wherein enthusiasts were few. Around the solemnly quiet rooms I would march with a catalogue, ticking those I liked, and condemning those that seemed feeble.

On one of these visits to the Grosvenor I spied a white kitten belonging to the cloakroom attendant. Noting my fervour, she offered to give it to me. Mother had no heart to refuse, and home it was taken, in a skewered fish-basket provided by the attendant. That journey home in the bus! The kitten wobbled about, pushing its nose almost through every weak spot in the basket. At every frantic mew there were pained looks from humane passengers, and mutters of 'Crool'. 'What shall we call it, Mother?' 'Sir Coutts Lindsey,' was the reply, because he had founded or presided over the Gallery. So Coutty was established with milk and buttered feet, and ruled the mice and us for several years. She must have been a tom, for she never produced any kittens, much to my disappointment.

Taking long walks in the country was the main relaxation in those days when even bicycles, or velocipedes as they were called, were rare enough to be stared at. My father's plan for a half-holiday when no cricket was to be had was usually to go with all the boys to Barnet or Potters Bar by train, and then walk far afield, twenty miles or more, returning dog-tired to a huge supper. Perhaps I was a bit envious of these outings. Whatever the reason, on one memorable day my father borrowed me, all alone, to go for a country walk with him. We started from Hampstead Heath Station as a base, and seemed to go a tremendous distance along lanes and across fields. I seized the chance to ask my father about his school-days. He could remember only two things about his boarding-school: one was that he had a barrel of apples sent him on a birthday, so heavy that it took two men to bring it in. The other memory was that he wrote home when he was twelve to say that he now knew quite enough, and might as well leave school. He laughed, but it seemed to me reasonable enough, for twelve was a big age, and he certainly knew everything. I believed all he said, and readily imagined that Gog and Magog came down to dinner every day in Guildhall when they heard the clock strike one, and even to this day I feel that guinea-pigs' eyes are not firmly set in their heads.

On this walk we grew very hungry, and then came the top of my pride and happiness, for we went into a little wayside inn with a sanded floor and sat in a parlour with coloured pictures and the sun coming in through a tiny window. Bread and cheese and beer were ordered! Well, if that wasn't being grown up and like the boys, what was? Beer tasted horrible to me as a rule, but this seemed ambrosial.

Barring such occasional jaunts to town or country, my mornings were 'busy', while Mother was light-heartedly painting. She said to me one day, 'Molly dear, I feel that I ought to be worrying.' 'What about, Mother?' 'Oh, nothing in particular, just worrying.'

The afternoons were my own, and I generally spent them in my own room. Here I was complete monarch. There was no attempt in those days to furnish a room to suit the occupant, and most of mine was taken up by a huge wooden bed and a huge chest of drawers. However, it had a jolly window looking down the street. As it was directly under the study, there was a chance for a postal system from one window to the other. A basket on a string would be let down by one of the boys and dangled in front of me. Pulling it in I would find a letter, asking me to fetch him a pair of scissors or a particular book. This I would find and place in the basket to be hauled up. Letters too of sheer camaraderie were passed to and fro, written on small fancy note-paper and envelopes. Several of these I still possess. The burden of most of them is a hope that I am quite well, but one begs me to take more than eighteenpence when I go to buy his (Barnholt's) birthday present, as 'there are some very fine stamp-albums to be got in the Upper Street for half-a-crown'.

As I lay awake in the morning I could see the houses opposite and a good bit of the street. I liked to hear the 'milk' cry of the women who carried the pails on yokes, and the cheery rat-tat of the postman, but the sweep's long-drawn wail used to fill me with misery when he made his rare rounds. One morning as I lay idly watching the house opposite I had one of the surprises of my life. A broom

*Portrait of a Young Girl, by Edward Robert Hughes*

suddenly shot out of a chimney. I never thought of connecting this fairy-tale event with the sweep, and thought Mother's explanation very dull. I ought to have asked my father.

Before I fell asleep at night I watched a room in the house opposite. All was rather vague until they lit up, and then there was glory. They were real people who walked about and talked and did things just like ourselves. But hardly had things begun to hum when some one would go and draw the curtains. This seemed heartless. Although Mother had curtains (for respectability, I suppose), she never drew them. 'If people like to look in,' she would say to visitors who remarked on the fact, 'they are quite welcome. I am not engaged in murder or coining, or anything that calls for reserve.'

Long afternoons I spent in my room alone, while the boys were at school.

Drawing and painting took most of the time, but there was also the curious occupation of cutting patterns in perforated cardboard, sticking them on a piece of coloured ribbon, and inflicting them on some aunts as a Bible bookmark. I had a boyish contempt for dolls, especially the flaxen-haired blue-eyed type, whose clothes wouldn't take off. These came in handy as an audience, for one of my favourite games was to hang over the foot of my bed, and preach to the counterpane, with a text duly given out twice, in different directions.

I must have done this to break the silence. No London child today can realize the quiet of the road on which my window looked. A tradesman's cart, a hawker or a hurdy-gurdy, were the sum total of the usual traffic. Sometimes everything had been so quiet for so long that the sound of a passer-by or of a butcher's pony would take on a distant, unreal tone, as if it were mocking me. This frightened me, and I would break the spell by singing 'The Lass of Richmond Hill'.

Music I made for myself with broken nibs stuck into the edge of my table. The tinkle was cheering, but no tune could I achieve, although Charles made effective ones on his 'organ' of nibs.

In spite of my contempt for dolls of the usual kind, and my intense hatred of sewing, I took great delight in dressing up the pawns of a very large set of chess-men, discarded by the family. White pawns became Arthur's knights or Greek heroes, as the fancy took me, black ones were pagans or Trojans. Bright bits of velvet and silk were sewn on them by my toiling fingers, and cardboard swords fitted to their sides. The best bits of stuff and passionate care were expended on Sir Lancelot, who slaughtered pagans with easy grace on my washing-stand.

Of course I had a shelf for my books. We were none of us too fond of showing our books to visitors. They didn't really care about them and sometimes would wet their fingers to turn over the pages. My own treasures are nearly all with me still, showing only the honourable marks of age and continual reading – no thumb-marks, no dogs' ears, no loose leaves. *Rosy's Voyage Round the World* was prime favourite. A little girl and three boys go out in a rowing-boat, sight Africa, find Crusoe's island, catch an eel, light a fire to cook it . . . and so on, in such a realistic way that I was as convinced of the extent of their travels as they were themselves. Each adventure had a full-page illustration by Lorenz Frolich. *The Little Gipsy*, also illustrated by him, was the story of an only child who is stolen by gipsies because of her lovely voice, brought up by them, and after terrible adventures becomes a famous singer and finds her parents. *Alice in Wonderland* we all knew practically by heart, and one of the red-letter days of my life was a birthday when I received from my father *Through the Looking-glass*. I got through the morning somehow, and then buried myself in it all the afternoon, my pleasure enhanced by the knowledge that there was a boring visitor downstairs to whom I ought to be making myself agreeable. And it was about chess-men! As I handle the book now I live over again that enchanted afternoon.

The pictures in our books were well drawn, but colour was very rare and highly prized. Just before the Christmas of 1872, Mother took me to Oxford Street to do some shopping. Our main object was to buy a birthday present for Charles. I can remember mounting the stairs at Bumpus's amid what seemed to me thousands of books – a land of Canaan indeed. The stairs are still there, and I prefer them to the lift, because they recall that golden day. Mother chose *The Story without an End*. The story itself was an allegory, and was too subtle for us, but it is impossible to describe the endless pleasure given us all by those full-page pictures, whose colours are as fresh and beautiful today as when Charles received them 'on his tenth birthday', as the inscription in Mother's handwriting records.

It was entirely due to its colour that another book became my constant companion. This was an illustrated Scripture text-book, given to me on my seventh birthday, and still preserved. I have never come across another like it. Some of the little pictures are very crude, but most of them, especially such short commands as 'Walk Honestly', 'Fear God', in fancy lettering, with gold and bright-coloured borders, are tasteful enough.

Many people of my age must have imbibed their early religious notions from the same book that I did – *The Peep of Day*, for my copy is dated 1872, and is one of the three hundred and forty-seventh thousand. It is very insistent and realistic about hell, and apparently there is only one virtue, obedience to parents and kind teachers, which leads of itself to a life of bliss 'beyond the sky'. One stanza of verse attracted me greatly:

> *Satan is glad – when I am bad,*
> *And hopes that I – with him shall lie*
> *In fire and chains – and dreadful pains.*

Whether the rhythm pleased me, or whether I was gratified that such an important person as Satan would actually welcome my company, I can't say, but the idea was more exciting than that of heaven put forth by the author. The stories about Jesus I liked best, and admired Him greatly. What a pity, I thought, that after such a good life He should have told an untruth at the last. This is what I read: 'Jesus just tasted the vinegar, and said, "It is finished."' My idea was that he had been given this horrid stuff to drink, tasted it, and then out of politeness pretended that he had finished it up.

I suppose that like all children I never asked any one about the things that really puzzled me, although I was ready enough to ask questions for the sake of asking. When obliged to sit and be polite listening to a visitor's conversation, I used to break the monotony with an innocent question, always prefaced by the phrase 'What means by?' Thus I would ask, 'What means by poison?' 'What means by lottery?' 'What means by jealous?' Mother would enter into explanations, only too thankful, I fancy, to find something to talk about. But one day she turned upon me, thoroughly exasperated, because I had asked, 'What means by Russia?' It seemed to me quite a promising opening, and I never knew why it suddenly enraged her.

Alone, in my room, I pondered over much. Once I was perturbed more seriously than a grown-up ever imagines. God had very kindly made the world, but suppose the notion had never occurred to Him? Suppose there had never been any God? Suppose there had never been anything at all? I was so devastated by the thought that I had to run about violently up and down stairs to kill the demon.

*Illustration to* ALICE THROUGH THE LOOKING-GLASS, *by John Tenniel*

*A Rest in Rotten Row, by Rose Maynard Barton*

# 6

# SUNDAY

HE mere word 'Sunday' is apt to give a mental shiver to people of long memories. The outer world closed down. It was wrong to travel except for dire necessity, and then very difficult. It was wrong to work, and wrong to play. In fact, existence in some houses was so dull that Tom said he understood the full meaning of the opening verse of the 122nd Psalm. However, we did the best we could with the day, and it had the advantage of my father being with us all the time. He didn't take religion *too* seriously, and left it to Mother to enforce all her superstitious restrictions that she had imbibed in her Cornish home.

She for her part put all the cheerfulness she could into the food, against which there seemed to be no Biblical taboo. Instead of the daily tea for breakfast we had coffee – lashings of real strong coffee, with a great jug of hot milk. When the season allowed we always had sausages ('the British weekly'). But while these appetizing smells were around us we had to learn the Collect and get it 'heard' before breakfast. One blessed Sunday after Trinity produced a Collect so free from fulsome flattery, so quick off the mark in its demands, that we learnt it in no time. Even now a Collect smells to me of coffee.

Breakfast over, the whole family walked in detachments to St Paul's Cathedral. We had reduced the route to a science, by side streets, short cuts by the New River, along parts of Essex Road, the City Road, Goswell Road, and Aldersgate, and finally past 'the highest point of London' in Panyer Alley to the north door of the cathedral. I must have been very little when I did this long walk, because I once described it as 'continully cwossing'. My father explained to me that the more slantingly you crossed a road the shorter it was. He also alleviated the walk by playing wayside cribbage, a favourite game in the country. In town the points for scoring had to be rather different; thus we had: man carrying baby, 5; three in a hansom, 5; perambulator, 1; cat in a window, 15; ladder, 1; man with a mourning hatband, 5; any one we knew to speak to (very rare), 31, game. I think we must have played this when Mother was walking behind, or this game would never have slipped through her rules.

*View of London from St Paul's, by T. Sulman*

Sometimes Mother and I went by tram, but the horse affair was so slow, the waiting for it so long, and the stoppings so frequent, that the walkers reached Aldersgate before we did. Occasionally my father would vary the route home by taking us through the deserted City, free of all traffic, and showing us Austin Friars and funny little passages, till we came to Broad Street and thence back to Canonbury by train.

How cool and vast the cathedral seemed after the dusty streets! We walked with precision to our special seats, for the vergers knew us well. My father had a stall, my brothers sat in a pew beyond the choir, my mother and I sat in the reserved front row under the dome. The cathedral seemed to belong to us, and little took place that escaped the notice of one or other of us.

I have wondered since those days why we all took those long walks through dull streets, and endured those long services. Not from pious or educative motives. It must have been simply for the inspiriting music that burst from that organ and that choir. It was worth all the endurance, even of the Litany. No footling sentimental hymns, but Te Deums, Psalms, Creeds, Introits, and Kyries that intoxicated us. During one boy's solo my father was so excited that his fist came thump down on his neighbour's shoulder. We children knew all the chants, and used often at home to converse loudly to their tunes. We had nicknames for our favourite Creeds. There was the 'trumpet' Creed, with six trumpet-notes on the organ before each section. We could rely on getting this on the great Feast days. Another was called the 'cup of tea' Creed, because the recurring theme was just the same as that of a comic song of the time, running:

*First you take and warm your teapot, let your water boiling be,*
*That's a most important secret, and see you do not spare the tea.*

Sermons, of course, were on the endurance side, but had some alleviations. I had a nice long sit down, and as I was always seated close to the pulpit I enjoyed the colours of the marble pillars, and could weave fancies round the Punjaub, a funny name to have on a pulpit. If the preacher grew fierce I looked at the statue of Samveli Johnson, whom I vaguely connected with Sam Weller, and if he were gentle I looked at the one of Howard with his keys, a satisfying face and figure. It is curious that during all those years I never inquired who these people were. The sermons were seldom less than three-quarters of an hour. To the preacher it was the chance of a lifetime. He would never again 'address London'. We got to be a little sorry for him as he went up the steps, conducted by the melancholy-looking verger who certainly must have given him a gloomy foreboding of his reception by 'London'. He did not know how his voice would carry under the dome, and we took joy in seeing whether he would bawl, or roar like any sucking dove.

During the summer months we had a series of colonial bishops, who told us all they had ever thought in their far-flung places. The only man we ever heard more than once was the Dean, who always preached on the great Feast days, and let us off with half an hour. The only sermon of his that I recall was a Christmas one, when he besought us to enjoy ourselves, dinner and all, because that was what the Lord would like best. 'A sprig of withered parsley' was the description of Dean Church by some wit of the day. He was a very slight, care-worn-looking man, ending the procession into the service, letting his board hang listlessly from his hand, mounting into his stall with a semi-detached air, as if the whole business was of little concern. For some reason we had boundless respect for him, and liked to hear him read the Gospel, in which the only word he ever emphasized was 'and'. The effect of this, strangely enough, was to give extraordinary dignity to the narrative of the passion.

The sermons were usually stiff with learning and far over our heads. After one on Solomon's vision, I asked Barnholt on the way home whether *he* would have chosen wisdom if he had been Solomon. 'Oh, no,' said he, 'I've got enough of that. I should have asked for a new cricket-bat.' The rest of the walk home was spent in enlarging on the things we might have got from such a golden opportunity.

Dinner-time on Sunday was the occasion for us all to compare notes and criticisms of the voices of canon, minor canon, and preacher, and the shade of ritualism of the stranger. Whether he stood at the north end of the altar, or in the middle – it was a burning question in those days, when clergymen were being imprisoned for Romish practices. We had no feelings in the matter, but we loved to see some one sailing near the wind.

The afternoons hung heavy. It seemed to be always 3 o'clock. All amuse-ments, as well as work, were forbidden. It was a real privation not to be allowed to draw and paint. However, an exception was made in favour of illuminated texts, and we rivalled the old monks in our zeal for copying Scripture, with the same kind of worldly decorations that they devised.

Naturally our main stand-by was reading, but here again our field was limited by Mother's notions of what was appropriate for Sunday. *Tom Brown*, *Robinson Crusoe*, Hans Andersen's *Tales*, and *Pilgrim's Progress* were permit-ted, but not the *Arabian Nights*, or Walter Scott, or indeed any novel. We had to fall back on bound volumes of *Good Words for the Young*, which were not so bad as the title suggests, and contained plenty of stories. Again and again I turned to something entitled *The Dark Journey*, only to find that it was an account of one's digestion. You may wonder why I did this more than once, but I always hoped that I had been mistaken, and that such a splendid title must mean a good story. No, there was still that forbidding picture of one's insides cut through the middle.

We all liked certain parts of a three-volume story called *Henry Milner*, which purported to be an account of the up-bringing of a Christian gentleman. I believe he never did anything wrong, but his school-fellows did, and all their gay activities shone like misdeeds in a pious world.

The Bible proved often more entertaining than the 'good' books. One day when Barnholt was desperate for a new story I recommended Esther as being as good as the *Arabian Nights*. He hung back, however, until I urged the point that God was not mentioned in it. 'No, really?' he cried, seized the Bible, and soon became absorbed in the plot. He and I used to gloat too over the horrors of the Revelation, more than over its brighter passages. One thing puzzled us: when the twenty-four elders had cast down their crowns, what happened next? Did they run and pick them up again to throw them down again, or were new crowns supplied to them?

Religious talk was seldom, if ever, inflicted on us. The question of conscience once arose when Mother was reading *Jessica's First Prayer* aloud to Barnholt and me. 'What means by conscience?' said I. 'Surely,' Mother replied in rather shocked tones, 'you have heard the voice of God speaking to you, and telling you not to do what is wrong?' Scenting danger, I hastily agreed. 'And you too, Barnholt, of course?' 'No,' said he, 'I've never heard any voice at all.' Mother pressed him, asserting that he *must* have heard it. But he stuck to his point, and how I admired him, and wished I had had the courage to say the same, because I had never heard anything either.

Sunday newspapers did exist, but were not respectable. How horrified my father was on discovering that the servants had been reading little bits to me out of *Lloyd's Weekly*! He gave me to understand that I must never read it because the small print was so bad for me. Now and again, however, I noticed on a Sunday walk that he bought a paper. For sometimes my father would cut out all church-going and announce, 'Let's go up to Hampstead Heath to see the sun shine.' We never gave him time to change his mind, or Mother's conscience a chance to get to work about Sunday travelling, but were soon hustling off with him to the station. Yes, the sun was shining on the heath sure enough, and we scampered about the wild paths that stretch beneath the group of firs by the *Spaniards*. Fifty years have made little difference to that scene. I think the very bench under the trees is the same, but the country lane that led to Highgate has been civilized into villadom and a good run for cars. Down Highgate Hill we ran, always paying our respects to Dick Whittington's stone on the way, took a tram along Holloway, and reached home with the appetites of hunters.

My father's Sunday efforts weakened towards evening, and after tea he liked to read aloud to us from books that sounded quite well, but afforded some chance of frivolity. Of course Shakespeare is Shakespeare, but we got boisterous joy out of Falstaff and his men in buckram, out of Hotspur's contempt for Glendower, and Fluellen's brush with Pistol over the leek. *Ingoldsby Legends* were always in demand, and above all the *Misadventures at Margate*, which we knew almost by heart. I took my cue from the boys and laughed whenever they did, but it was not till much later in life that I perceived the humour of what was read. Never mind, I was led to welcome a joke as though it were a jewel, and the mere habit has made life jollier. One thing over which they laughed did, however, worry me. The closing couplet of the Margate poem was so easy to understand, and so silly. How could any one be so foolish as to ring a bell, have the door answered, and then have nothing to say but that a friend of his was pretty well?

*Pickwick Papers*, by some blessed workings of Mother's conscience, did not come under the head of novels. They were 'papers'. She herself led the laughter over the long gamekeeper and Bob Sawyer's supper-party. Not sabbatical by any means, but those readings rescued our childhood's Sundays from the grimness that might otherwise have stuck to them. And often my father would read us things that he loved, without a single word of 'explanation'. Of these the *Ancient Mariner* stands out beyond the rest. O happy living things! Why do people murder them by explanations?

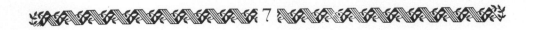 

# 7

# A LONG RAILWAY JOURNEY

OUR lack of interest in kinsfolk and acquaintance in London was more than balanced by our enthusiasm for our relations in Cornwall.

Mother's family was not only numerous and well-to-do, but intelligent and jolly. Hardly a year passed but some of us paid them a visit, and occasionally it was all of us. Among, then, the bits of luck in my childhood must be included this plunge from London to the depth of the country.

To us children an important element in this piece of luck was the journey of three hundred miles that it involved. Our parents must have thought otherwise. Had they not been peculiarly care-free by disposition they would never have embarked on the adventure of taking five children all that way in a train of the 'seventies. Coaching days were doubtless bad, but there were inns on the way.

We used to go to bed earlier the day before, not so much to please Mother as to bring tomorrow a bit sooner. We got up long before it was necessary, impeding all the sandwich-making and hard-boiling of eggs that was going on. But eat a good breakfast we could not, being 'journey-proud', as our old cook used to express our excited state. Meanwhile the luggage was being assembled in the hall, having its last touches of cording and labels. For weeks I had been packing in my bedroom, and once I presented five large cardboard boxes, wobbly with various belongings. My father ran upstairs to inspect them, and solemnly looking at them said, 'Now, Molly, which of these is really the most important?' Charmed by his business-like manner and by the word 'important', I gladly pointed to one, and consented to leave the others behind.

The next crisis was the fetching of a cab. At 7 o'clock in the morning there was no certainty of getting one quickly, and we kept rushing to the window until some one shouted, 'Here it comes.' If you saw that cab today your anxiety would be as to whether it could possibly stay the course to Paddington. The few 'growlers' still to be seen in the London streets are royal coaches compared with those of the 'seventies. They were like the omnibuses, with the same dingy

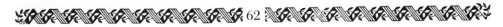

blue velvet, only much dirtier, and as they were used for taking people to hospitals my father used to call them 'damned fever-boxes'. To us children, no Cinderella's fairy-carriage could have been handsomer than the cab actually at the door. If we were all going my father and the elder boys had to follow in a second cab. Luggage was piled on the top, and we were packed in among rugs, umbrellas, and hand-bags. At last the cabby climbed up to his seat and whipped up the horse. It took an hour or more to jog along from Canonbury to Paddington, but we did reach the enchanted spot at last.

The train was scheduled to start at 9 a.m. and to arrive at Camborne at 9 p.m. This was before the days of the Flying Dutchman, not to mention the Cornishman and the Riviera Express. Even when the Flying Dutchman was begun it had no third class, and was too expensive for the whole family. Luncheon-baskets had not been invented, neither was it possible to reserve seats. In order, therefore, to travel all together in one compartment we had to arrive more than half an hour before the train was to start. There was then the suspense of waiting for it to come in, and my fear that we might not be on the right platform or that the Great Western had forgotten all about it. My father meanwhile was taking the tickets and having the luggage labelled. Never did he hasten his steps or hurry, no matter what the emergency, so that there was the additional fear that he would miss the train. When at last we were all safely in a carriage, he would saunter off to buy a paper, and other people were coming in.

In time everything was settled and we were gliding out, 'with our faces towards Cornwall', as Mother used to say. Very little of the view from the windows escaped us, and I was privileged to 'kneel up' and report the latest news to the company. No sooner had we fairly left London behind, were gathering speed, and had sated ourselves with fields and hedges for a while, than we began to survey our fellow passengers and make friends with them. In the old broad-gauge carriages there were usually six a side, and much courtesy was needed for a long run when there was no escape from one another. Our parents took care to found a family tradition of being good travellers, which was understood to mean that we must not be a nuisance to other people, by crowding the window, talking loudly, moving about, eating before the appointed time (and perhaps being ill) . . . and the evil-doings of children who began to eat sweets before Reading were pointed out.

Where we came out strong in the carriage company at large was in our superior familiarity with the route. We knew all the points of interest to be looked out for. 'We are going to Cornwall.' 'We always go there.' 'We'll show

*A Station Refreshment-Room*

*Rain, Steam and Speed – The Great Western Railway, by J.M.W. Turner*

you when it comes.' By such delicate expressions of superiority we managed to conceal our contempt for the poor creatures who 'were only going to Bristol', or some degraded person who had to 'change at Didcot'. What we most liked was a grown-up, preferably a man, who was a complete stranger to the line. A kindly clergyman would listen with apparent fervour to our informative talk about Brunel and the viaducts, or be shown the 'very place that Turner took for his "Rain, Steam and Speed"'. We knew the exact point to get a view of Windsor Castle, and showed it as if it were our own.

Reading, the first stop, was great fun for those on the near side. What more cheering than to see distracted people looking for seats when we were definitely full up? If we had a vacant seat at any stop Charles would suggest that I should be pushed forward, for any one on seeing me, he maintained, would try farther on. Or he would ejaculate, as any one was about to come in, 'No one would think that Barnholt was recovering from measles!' We talk of the confusion of a modern station, but it is orderly peace compared to the rushing about and shouting of those days. The wonder is that we ever moved on again. And yet we didn't dare to leave the carriage, because at any moment the guard might decide that he had had enough.

Didcot had one definite pleasure. We knew that little boys would be going up and down the platform singing out, 'Banbury cakes! Banbury cakes!' And Mother would crane out and buy some, just to encourage the crew.

Next came Swindon – name of sweet assurance. How often Mother used to say, 'They *can't* leave Swindon under ten minutes, no matter how late we are.' Considering our early breakfast, or lack of it, the refreshment-room at Swindon was a land of Canaan, and the hot soup all round is still a joyful memory. So hot it was that Dym launched a theory that it was hoped some would be left to serve up for the next train. Those ever-memorable ten minutes were no doubt entirely for the gain of the restaurant and entirely to the detriment of the Great Western, but they were sheer life-savers to long-distance travellers. In later years the railway had to compensate the restaurant for doing away with those ten minutes, to the tune of £50,000. Perhaps a little remorseful, the restaurant proprietors presented a silver model engine to Swindon, to commemorate the transaction, and the little model is known to the railwaymen as 'the £50,000 engine'.

Thus refreshed we were all agog for our next excitement – the Box Tunnel. The railway cuttings grew higher and higher, and at last we rushed with a piercing whistle into the total darkness of 'the longest tunnel in the world'. The oil lamps, and later the gas lamps, were let down from above with much labour only at dusk. There was no thought of lighting up for a tunnel. Old ladies may have been afraid of robbery and murder, but it was a great feature of the day's entertainment to us. By a pre-arranged plan the boys and I rose stealthily and felt our way into one another's places. When the train emerged into the light the elders sustained a turn, or handsomely pretended that they did.

The charm of Bristol was its appearance of being a half-way house. Not that it was so by any means, but it was the elbow-joint in the journey. The muddle and rush were greater even than at Reading, and we were often kept there for some twenty minutes. Yet we dared not leave the carriage for more than a mere leg-stretch just outside the door. I sucked much pleasure from hanging out at the off-side window, to watch the man tapping the wheels and applying the yellow stuff from his box. Thus I understood what my father meant by calling London butter 'train-oil'.

Some of our company usually left the train at Bristol, so that we had the carriage more or less to ourselves, and could move about more freely. This was specially desirable because there was soon to come a magic moment when a glimpse of the sea was possible, just for the short time when Bridgwater Bay was visible on our right. Then we bowled along the warm sleepy countryside of Somerset, with no excitements beyond fields and cows and tiny villages, mile after mile. This was the strategic point that Mother chose for unveiling dinner. A bulging basket had long been eyed as it sat in the rack. Restaurant cars are boons, and luncheon-baskets have their merry surprises, but for food as a species of rapture nothing compares with sandwiches, eggs, pasties, and turnovers, doled out one by one from napkins, when the supply is severely limited. Oranges in summer were unknown then, as well as all the foreign apples and other fruit to be had in London today. We had to slake our thirst with acid-drops and a tiny ration of lemonade. If by chance a fellow passenger remained we always managed to do some little barter of biscuits or sweets, because strange food is even more pleasant than one's own.

We used to hail Exeter as being 'almost there', for it was in Devon, actually the next county to Cornwall, and definitely 'west'. A quiet dignity pervaded its saintly stations, but we could never stay long because of course we were late. A train in those days was never 'on time'. After Exeter we were all keyed up for the greatest treat of the journey. I have travelled in many show places of Europe and America, but have never been along a piece of line to equal the run from Exeter to Teignmouth. We children were not stirred as Mother was by the beauties of the estuary and the opposite shore. What we looked out for were the waders carrying on some mysterious hunt in the water, and two pleasure-boats, shaped like some kind of water-fowl, and called the *Swan* and *Cygnet*. I never dreamt but what they were real birds.

Then, with a magnificent gesture, the Great Western swept us to the sea-side, indeed almost into the sea. Mother remembered a day when the waves had washed into the carriage. The bare possibility of such a thing made this part of the run something of an adventure, and we almost hoped it would happen again.

The sun was always shining at Dawlish, and there was the sea all spread out in dazzling blue. And as if the train knew how to enhance the effect, it would roll in and out of short tunnels in the 'rouge' or red sandstone of Devon. Each time it emerged the sea looked bluer and the rocks more fantastic in shape. However beautiful the inland scenery might be, it seemed dull after this, and after Teignmouth we usually fell asleep. I remember being laid out at length with my head on Mother's lap, and the rest being a blank till the glad sound of 'Here's Plymouth' woke me.

By now it was late afternoon, and you would suppose that here at last would be some chance of tea and a wash in comfort. Ah no! The London train didn't care about Cornwall, there were no through carriages arranged for long-distance people, and we had to change into a local affair, with hard wooden seats, and patronized by a succession of market people with large bundles. By the time we had found this train, seen the luggage shifted, carried along our small parcels, and settled into our seats, there was no time to do more than buy a bag of buns. They had not thought then of allowing people to carry cups of tea into the carriage with them.

In all this confusion I had time to notice that we were coming out of Millbay the same way that we had gone in. It was a sort of terminus, apparently, and very mysterious, because I was assured that we were not going back to London. I asked my father what became of the engine that had brought us from London. How did it get out so as to pull the train away again? He explained very carefully how it was lowered into an underground passage, run along under the train, and then hauled up again at the other end. This seemed to me no more peculiar than most things.

Shipping on the Hamoaze amused us mightily enough until we reached the climax of our journey – the Albert Bridge. We were leaving 'England' behind and were in the enchanted land of Cornwall at last. We greeted the tiny whitewashed cottages of the 'natives' with far greater fervour than we had shown over Windsor Castle. We vied with one another in trying to remember the order in which the stations came. We stopped at all of them. And when I say stopped I mean stopped. There was none of the hurry of Reading or Bristol. We leant out to catch the accents of the porter, proclaiming his piece in the soft west-country drawl. We watched all the greetings and partings and waving of hands of the travellers . . . Then would descend that peculiar silence of a country station that signifies that every one is settled, and the guard feels that it is safe to let the train start again.

If a sun-bonneted market woman got in with us Mother could never resist talking to her, and answering the invariable Cornish question 'Wheer be 'ee goin'?' Then would follow the astonished 'From Lunnon, are 'ee? Aw, my deer!'

And now it was growing dusk, and the familiar tin-mine buildings were silhouetted against the sky, and generally darkness had descended before we ran into Camborne more than an hour late. We had become indescribably dirty and tired and hungry. But our reception atoned for all. Countless uncles and aunts and cousins were crowding the platform, and as we got out every one was exclaiming 'Here they are!' We children were the heroes and the spoilt darlings of the hour. We were bundled into waiting carriages and driven to a

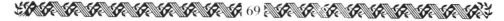

*View from the Balcony, by Albert Goodwin*

royal spread. On one such occasion I remember my cousin Edgar running all the mile and a half by the side of the carriage in the dark, giving us a whoop of joy when a gate into a lane had to be opened for us to pass.

# 8

# RESKADINNICK

SUCH was the name of the homestead that was our journey's end. To any but a Cornishman the word sounds strange. London trades-people made curious play with it, and Peter Robinson once sent a parcel to my aunt addressed: 'Miss Vivian, c/o Rev. Kadinnick.' To us children the name was synonymous with Paradise.

I call it a homestead because it was much more than a mere home or house or farm. When the town was left behind you entered a lane through a gate. This had the alluring name of Blackberry Lane, and meandered between mossy hedges thick with wild flowers until a large white gate barred the way. Beyond this was a quarter of a mile of sweeping drive, bordered by neatly cut grass and tall trees of great variety with more woodland behind them. Here and there was a bright flowering shrub, and in one recessed spot was a deep pond among the trees. A beautiful cool walk on a summer's day, but terrifying at night when one had to come home alone in the dark.

With the last curve of the drive the house came in sight, facing a large lawn, bordered by wooded banks and dotted with huge elms. While the carriage-drive led away through another wood to a lane beyond, a flower-garden lay on the other side of the house. Over a little brook and up a sunny bank there stretched a kitchen garden with fruit-trees innumerable, and in another part was a special orchard.

My grandfather had planned the whole place and planted all the trees except two Scotch firs in the drive, of unknown antiquity. The house too was of his own building, arranged for his bride in the reign of George III.

He had started with a farm and its dwelling-house, with huge old outside chimneys, gables, rafters, and stone floors. The walls were made of anything to be had some two or three centuries ago — mostly mud and timber. In some alterations made during my time a large trunk of a tree was found embedded in one wall. In some places these walls were two yards thick, and it had been customary to gouge a bit out when a cupboard was wanted.

At the end of this old part he had built a new Georgian house, with pillared

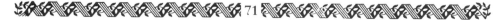

front and a brick arch at each side, concealing the back regions. These arches became mellowed in colour and creeper-clad, and gave a pleasant surprise to any one approaching and passing through to the beautiful older buildings beyond.

The connection of the new house with the old had necessitated some strange staircases and dark corners, and every room seemed to lead into some other room. And it was easy to get on the roof, or jump from a window at almost any point. The delightfully rambling *ensemble* seemed to have been designed by some celestial architect for the sole purpose of playing hide-and-seek. My grandfather had ten children, and no doubt they took as much advantage of this as we grandchildren did.

The out-buildings were even more rambling and mysterious than the interior. Beyond the great dairy there was the hen-yard, surrounded by coops inhabited by hens in every stage of their duty. From this you went into the big yard, with its long row of stables and a granary over them. Beyond this again was the lower yard, where the cows were housed and milked in sheds all round, and where the pigs wallowed about in the middle. By the side of this was the big barn, and beyond that the 'mowey', another yard where the ricks were built up on stone supports to keep the rats away. The little lane led in one direction to the smithy, the horse-pond, and a few scattered cottages, and in the other direction to the water-mill. All round were the various fields belonging to the farm, some with cows, some with sheep, but most of them with corn.

The difficulty on arriving from London was to know where to begin enjoying oneself. I well remember one such evening, being far too excited to sleep, I kept leaping from my bed to the window-seat, from sheer exuberance. At last I burst one of the panes in pieces. My golden aunt thought this quite a natural thing to do, and 'it saved having to open the window'.

As a regular thing so far as I was concerned the first charge on the estate was a personal visit to every animal. Cats first. These were divided into four distinct classes, and the cats seemed to be as snobbish as humans. The parlour cats were Persians, sat on laps and best chairs, and would never recline in the kitchen, although they would stroll casually about when a savoury smell was prevailing. The kitchen cats seemed to be always having kittens in the fathomless linen-cupboard at the top of the stairs. If they ventured into the dining-room it was to hide under the table in the hope of gain. Orchard cats prowled round the yards and stables, quite self-supporting, never venturing indoors unless under stress of hunger. One of these, a tom called Sarah, was so fierce that I was afraid to stroke him, and threw scraps to him at a distance. Then there were the office cats. The 'office' was a side wing of the old house, where accounts were kept and where the farm-men used to be paid on a Saturday. Behind it was a place called the 'slaughter-house', which I never had the courage to explore; the name put me off. A few cats, lean and humble-minded, managed to exist in this borderland, despised by both parlour and kitchen cats.

The only creature that really frightened me was the turkey-cock. Nothing in my life has ever made me so weak with terror as that horrible gobbling bird. Tired of parading with his harem in the orchard, he would now and again strut in the hen-yard or mowey. He would definitely forbid me to cross a yard if he was in it. If I made a dash to cross it, so would he . . .

There was never any alarm to me about a horse, and the very smell of the stables was intoxicating. Beautiful, glossy-coated carriage-horses, a pony for us to ride, and numberless farm-horses – all were beloved. One of these last was called Taffy, an enormous fellow, noted for his ferocity. At dinner one day I was missing, and as children never fail to turn up at meal-time unless something has gone wrong, a search was ordered. I could be found in none of the usual haunts, and as I was only five years old, anxiety began. At last I was discovered seated cross-legged, with complete unconcern, under Taffy, who was munching from his manger. The stable-boy who accidentally found me had to entice me away, for he was afraid to go near Taffy himself.

Only one dog do I remember. I think he was so dear to every one that when he died the family could never bear to have another. Theo was a great shaggy Newfoundland, who joined in all our childish games as well as ever he could, being treated as a member of the family. The old cook was heard to say one day, as she stooped to pick up his dish, 'Have you finished, please, Master Theo?' Barnholt once offered him a bite of his bun, but Theo did not quite understand the limits implied in the word 'bite', and the whole bun disappeared.

With such profusion of cows, sheep, pigs, poultry, and vegetation of all kinds, Reskadinnick was practically self-supporting, and my grandfather was able to boast frequently that there was nothing on the dinner-table but what he had produced on the farm. Fish was a rare treat, and a gift of trout or salmon was prepared and served with a ritual almost religious. Now and again there would resound from the lane a penetrating cry of 'Pilchards! Pilchards!' There had been a big haul, and a pony-cart was going round the countryside to sell them. All other food-preparations were then set aside for a pilchard orgy. The

*Bread Winners, by Walter Langley*

staple food was 'pig-meat' in its endless variety, and poultry. We had an old cookery-book containing this, to a London mind, extraordinary hint: 'If you have nothing in the house, and company should come, take a cold turkey, &c.' To suggest the killing and cooking of a live turkey is reasonable enough, but to select a cold one from one's 'empty' larder!

Bread was made every day, in batches of a dozen manchet loaves. A 'manchet' was a loaf moulded by hand, and not put in a tin. It was against ancient ritual for a loaf that had been cut to be placed on the table. My aunt was so angry one day when this occurred that I began to wonder what became of all the bread that was left. However, the mystery was solved when I saw her preparing a mash for the turkeys. In my day German yeast was used, but Mother told me that when she was little they had no yeast, but used a bit of the dough of the previous batch to raise the new batch. What puzzled her so much was how they ever *began* it. Probably she asked and no one knew, for like so many Cornish customs it may have been centuries old, and I picture the Phoenicians bringing a piece of dough as a capital invention of the East. They used to bake the loaves, Mother told me, by placing them in the wood-ash on the great stone slab in the kitchen. The stone slab is still there, and I have often stood on it and looked up the great chimney to the open sky. How jolly, I thought, those old wood fires must have been, with their spits and their cauldrons, so much more fun than the iron range, which in its turn seems fun compared to my modern efficient gas-stove.

The centre of excitement in the food scheme was the dairy. Its stone floor and slate shelves made it cool on the hottest day. On the shelves were ranged vast pans of milk, in various stages from cow to consumer. Foaming in from the milking-sheds, standing for the cream to rise before being scalded, scalded and thick with the deep cream waiting to be skimmed (the most attractive form), scalded and allowed to be drunk *ad lib.*, sold to children at the door for a halfpenny a quart, or more often given to them for nothing. Now I had a special and private permit from my aunt to go into the sacred dairy and help myself to the clotted cream whenever I liked.

The bulk of the cream was, of course, turned into butter. Turned, not churned. A churn was never seen at Reskadinnick. It had been heard of, and actually used by my aunt who lived up in the town, but Tony, my golden aunt of Reskadinnick, tossed her head at the idea. She had her own ritual of butter-making, and many a time I used to curl up in the corner of the kitchen window-seat to watch it. Her hands had to be elaborately washed first, and dipped in cold water to be cool. The wooden tub with the cream in it had to be held at a special angle on her lap. With fixed eye and stern mouth she then began to swirl the cream round, and you mustn't speak to her till the butter 'came'. One day I was allowed as a great treat to make a little butter all by myself, with no one even watching. When it 'came', behold, it was very good, and the joy of creation was mine.

Disapproval, of course, among the severer grown-ups. It was mad to let the child try such things. She might have wasted it all. But Tony was all for letting the children do and see and try things. I was wakened one night by a figure standing over me with a candle. It was Tony. 'Come along,' said she, picking me up and carrying me out pick-a-back, 'we are going to see the glow-worms.' And sure enough she carried me along the drive in my nightdress, to a spot where the worms were shining, and the elders gathered round admiring them. The child didn't catch her death, as was gloomily hoped by the disapproving, but lived to be always grateful for that only chance that has ever come her way of seeing a glow-worm.

Sanitation was not known at Reskadinnick, neither earth nor water nor any such thing. A huge tub collected the rain-water, of which there was never any shortage, and in this we washed. I had never seen a bathroom, even in London, let alone in Cornwall. A tin bath was kept in each bedroom. In the rain-water was a good deal of livestock wriggling about, but we got used to this. Our drinking-water was grand, coming from a spring in the lane.

Windows were made to open more or less, but they didn't matter much, because all through the day everybody was in and out at the ever-open doors, and in the evening when the family settled down 'to unbend over a book' every opening was shut tight. 'Night air' and 'such a draught' were considered 'enough to breed the cholera'. Our light was from candles and paraffin-lamps. Mother told me how magical it seemed to her when she first came to London to see some one turn a tap and produce a light at once from gas. She had heard how the 'best' people in London stood out against gas as being vulgar, and that Grosvenor Square was the last place to adopt it.

In spite of primitive conditions and stuffy nights, no one ever seemed to be ill. I never saw a doctor there, or heard the name of one, or heard Mother speak of one in earlier days. The older people all lived to great ages, and Uncle Bill reached a hundred. Up to his last few days he could swing along without a stick. He had travelled extensively, even to Greenland, but was born and died at Reskadinnick.

All this travelling of Uncle Bill and my grandfather was for mine-prospecting. Farming was not their main interest. Tin was everything, and it was as tin-mine managers and large shareholders that they made their wealth; and the management of the farm fell to a younger son, Joe.

The chief person round whom the whole establishment revolved was my aunt, always called Tony. Ever since her mother's death she had been mistress of the house. Not only did she manage every detail of the dairy, the poultry, and the work of the servants, but she was also widely read, an accomplished musician, a witty letter-writer, and above all an entrancing teller of stories. Her peculiar charm consisted in her greater delight in the doings of others than in her own. We children loved her, I think, better than our own mother.

It was from Mother that I learnt her story. Among my grandfather's travels was a visit to Norway, in connection with a purchase of timber for the mines. He took with him, just for the fun of it, his two eldest girls, my mother and Tony. The port for Norway had to be reached by coach, and this, with the putting up at inns and the voyage in a sailing-vessel, provided plenty of adventure. Their host was a Norwegian named Barnholt, a timber-merchant on a large scale, with one son, named Otto. The visit was made the occasion for excursions up country, mountaineering, driving, riding, and sailing on the fjords. When the time came for the return to Cornwall Otto had lost his heart to Tony.

Not long afterwards Otto's father died, leaving him to carry on the business of trading with England in timber. Nothing ever went wrong with his vessel, and in his anxiety to be a little richer before his marriage he stopped paying the insurance. On the very next voyage she was lost. Utterly broken in spirit Otto died soon afterwards, and Tony never got over her grief. She had plenty of admirers and appeared to enjoy life to the full, but froze up if any one approached the idea of marriage. All her wealth of affection was poured out on us children, and more especially on Barnholt, who was Otto's godson. She was the familiar friend, too, of all the cottage children for miles around, who would do anything for 'Miss Tony'. She had learnt to speak Norsk, and taught me to repeat little verses in it. It was one of my greatest treats to come into her bedroom and be shown some of the endless treasures she had collected. Among these was a baby shoe of Barnholt's with a hole worn in its sole.

I may add here that she lived to old age, full of humour and gaiety to the last. But shortly before her death she mentioned casually in a letter to me that the one thing she could never thank God for was her creation. I understood then how much a woman can hide.

Some years before my memory runs, Uncle Bill had brought his wife and three children back to Reskadinnick to stay, and there they remained permanently. So there was no lack of inmates. My special chum was Wilhelmina, or Mina, a girl of my own age. Mina's mother was an aunt of the severe type, in whose presence we were reticent about our escapades. Aunt Knight feared accidents, feared improprieties, feared (of all the absurdities) ill effects from non-stop apple-eating. One thing I shall never forgive her to my dying day: she got wind that Mina and I were riding home from a field on the top of the hay-wagons, and forbade it with such gestures of horror that we were actually alarmed into obedience. For us the wine of life was spilt for the whole hay season. However, she could be kindness itself when things went really wrong. When some little accident did occur, it was just as she had predicted, and one of her rare smiles appeared as she brought forth bandages and things. One day my pony, empty-saddled, came galloping home along the drive. A stirrup had broken and I had been thrown. Aunt Knight looking out of the window straightway swooned, and had to be given restoratives in early Victorian style. Her handwriting was exactly like Queen Victoria's, and she always crossed her letters. She swept about in black silk, had texts hung up in her bedroom, and shook her head with disapproval at any gaiety. I made Tony laugh by telling her that Aunt Knight was like Dogberry: 'If a merry meeting may be wished, God prohibit it.' As for a funeral anywhere about, it was nuts and figs, she was sure to have heard a dog howl, an owl hoot, or a bird flutter in the chimney, and consequently knew that something would happen. If Sirius were shining brightly it meant that Hell was very full.

Christianity did not seem to have penetrated Cornwall much. The Wesleyans were full of salvation and blood, but respectable Church people upheld Old Testament morality, with only lip-service to the New. Tony told me one day that she thought the New Testament was very dull compared to the Old. One Victorian custom which my father (God bless him!) had never even contemplated, was always observed at Reskadinnick. Family prayers, which my dear old grandfather had treated sketchily, were carried out by Uncle Bill with relentless thoroughness. Instead of mumbling a few simple requests to the Almighty, as grandpapa did, he acquired a book which covered the whole nation in its petitions, and even, on Fridays, went the length of praying for foreigners. All the servants were assembled, and it was morning *and* evening. As Lord Melbourne remarked, religion was threatening to invade the sanctity of private life. Perhaps he referred to Wesleyanism, for I must say that we had no more thrust upon us, except going to church on Sunday. In spite of Uncle Bill's long prayers, I heard him say one day that he thought it *wrong* to pray for anything except courage to meet whatever came.

*An Apple Orchard, by E.N. Downard*

Our parish church was at Penponds, a village some two miles away. The dear old parson was a survival of the eighteenth-century type, who took his duties lightly. His sermons were so few that Tony said she knew them all by heart and needn't attend to them. This was as well, for her energy was completely absorbed in keeping the school children decently behaved. To us London children the whole service seemed light comic opera after the austerities of St Paul's. Of course we never had the Litany, and the old chap would gabble through the alternate verses of the Psalms as fast as he could, followed by the hurried mumblings of the little congregation. All was simple and quickly over. On Communion Sunday (a very rare affair) matters were equally simple. Tom once 'stayed', and heard the pop of the cork as the parson opened the bottle of wine just before it was wanted.

Sundays on the whole were very jolly in Cornwall, if it hadn't been for the best clothes and the wearing of gloves. On account of these we couldn't pursue the usual plan of walking along the tops of the hedges. To those who don't know Cornwall I must explain that the hedges there are made of stones and earth, are thick with wild flowers, ivy, and ferns, and are just wide enough on the top to allow any one to walk unsteadily. Mina and I used to take one each side of a lane, and race each other along. Naturally this involved several falls and scrambling up again – not the best thing for Sunday clothes.

In the afternoons we unbelted and lay under the trees with any books we could find. My eldest cousin Beatrice was serious-minded like her mother, and attempted now and again to hold a Sunday School, and teach Mina and me something out of the Bible. But out of doors, as of course we were, the Bible somehow seemed funny, and the idea petered out.

In addition to the uncles, aunts, and cousins already mentioned there was another large family in the town about two miles away, and the coming and going was so unremitting that one hardly knew who belonged where. Sometimes even before breakfast a detachment of Uncle Joe's children would be seen coming round the last bend of the drive, full of expectancy that there would be something up.

And there always was.

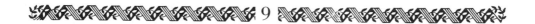 

# 9

# OUTDOOR DOINGS

'ESS me! D'ess me now! D'ess me *deckly* now!' According to tradition these were my words, accompanied by a stamp of my foot, as I stood at the top of the stairs one morning in my nightdress. I had overslept for once, and was frantic at having missed an hour of life. Not a moment's boredom did any of us know, but our programme depended a lot on the weather. Uncle Bill had a trying habit of tapping a kind of clock in the hall and telling us that it was going down. It surely must have gone up sometimes, in order to go down so persistently, but he never reported it. Then some wise grown-up would openly rejoice: rain was good for the garden or the tin-streams or something. However, by and by would come Uncle Joe on his horse, with a broad smile and distinct observations of blue sky in the right quarter.

Enough for us, and the glad cry of 'cliffs' would go round. Within an hour of the children's fiat Tony had packed our baskets, having duly looked round to see how many heads to count. Pretty heavy those baskets were, for in addition to the dinner they contained sketching-materials, bathing-gowns and towels, and often a book or two. However, the boys took it in turn to carry them, and the girls took sticks, spratting-hooks, and cans for possible treasures.

In twos and threes we straggled along our two-mile walk to the cliffs, a gradual rise all the way, chiefly across fields. We had no glimpse of the sea at any time until we were right at the top of the cliffs. We generally ran the last hundred yards or so, impatient for the glory that we knew to be there for us. That last lap was along a grassy path running through a stretch of purple heather. Then we saw the sea. Not the tame affair that you get at the 'sea-side', but a vast expanse of ultramarine and emerald, and far, far below, the roar of the breakers booming in and dashing their foam against the dark rocks, and the white flashing of the sea-gulls screaming to welcome us.

However, we were not there to admire – we were for the sea itself. And how to get down there? Had we been strangers we should have been afraid to attempt such a precipitous descent, but none of us could remember a time when it was not as familiar and friendly as the drive. We all plunged at once down a narrow path, a mere sheep-track, among the rocks and heather, scrambling and slithering and sliding, clutching at bushes or digging our spratting-hooks into the earth, till we reached at last a big platform of rock, from which we made a triumphal leap into the deep, soft sand.

Fortunately grown-ups never came with us, or they would have had heart-attacks, or, worse still, would have kept warning us not to slip. Our fearlessness was our safety. Once within a few yards of the sea, our things were off in a twinkling, and into the great pools we splashed. No one dreamt of venturing into that boiling, thundering, open sea, for its perils were too obvious. After about an hour of playing games in the pools, jumping from rock to rock, collecting anemones, shells, and seaweed for our cans, we clothed ourselves again, all except our feet which were bare till the final climb, and flocked round my eldest cousin, Beatrice, who dispensed the dinner. Our first course was always a pasty. I wonder who invented that perfectly complete and portable meal: a round of pastry doubled over contained fresh rump steak, and slices of potato well seasoned, and when baked became a juicy blend, but not too juicy to be grasped in the hand and nibbled away bit by bit, requiring neither knife nor fork. Then we all chased away to find a jolly place to sit, or to go on pursuing our private ends. Thirst soon brought us to Beatrice again, who doled out lemonade or cider. Then there was seed-cake for the still hungry, and plenty of apples.

After this we usually paddled and scrambled our way among the boulders to the next place along the shore that gave a possibility of climbing up again. About half-way up we would rest on some grassy shelf of the cliffs and follow our particular bent. Charles and Beatrice and I did some painting, others would merely watch the sea for distant steamers. No boats of any kind could come near that coast. My cousin Lucy had a passion for the sea, and never forgave Providence for not making her a boy. She had several blue-jackets to whom she wrote every month in connection with Miss Weston's Mission, and from their replies she would spin us yarns, or tell us bits out of *Tom Cringle's Log*, and incidentally teach us nautical phrases and how to tie knots.

After the last lap of our long climb to the top we used to enjoy walking along the grassy path among the heather that skirted the edge of the cliff, every now and again dangerously near. At one point this led to 'Hell's Mouth', quite the most attractive spot in the world. It was a deep cove that could not be approached from the shore, and into which no boat could enter without being dashed to pieces. We used to crawl up to the overhanging edge on all fours, lie full length, and gloat with fearful pleasure at the scene below, where the great waves would swirl in on their ugly business, and presently dash out with triumphant roar and splash of spray. Lucy had blood-curdling tales of human bones down there, of people who had fallen down, or, more darkly, been pushed. I have had to come away hurriedly, understanding Horatio's words:

> *The very place puts toys of desperation*
> *Without more motive into every brain*
> *That looks so many fathoms to the sea*
> *And hears it roar beneath.*

On the way home we wandered about the fields, gathering any spoil we could find to take home to Tony – blackberries, mushrooms, wild flowers. She welcomed everything, but her first demand was always, 'Show me your sketches.' If sea and rocks proved too maddeningly difficult we fell back on a drawing of Carn Brea, a kind of local Fuji-Yama or holy hill. Tony paid us the compliment of severe criticism. To one of my attempts she said, 'Heather, dear? Oh . . . I thought it was an impression of the field of Waterloo after the battle.'

Perhaps it was the tea at the end that was the best part of the day. Like Mother, Tony firmly believed in a spread on our return. There were splits and butter, apple cake, saffron cake, and lashings of cream. By the way, both in Cornwall and London jam was practically unknown to us, and what we saw of it in other houses we didn't like. Alice's 'jam every other day' carried no fun for me. Now if it had been 'apple cake every other day' I should have understood. This was made by filling a plate with pared apples, covering it with a round of pastry, baking it, reversing the crust, sugaring the apple, and spreading it over the crust. When cold, cream is added if you've got it. There was a lifelong feud between two of my aunts, because on one occasion the apple cakes had been salted instead of sugared, and each one declared it was the other who had done it.

When the big expedition to the North Cliffs was not on the cards, there were plenty of other pursuits in the place itself. There were two or three ponds, and a pond has great possibilities. One of these was cunningly placed in the side garden among tall elms inhabited by cawing rooks. Reflections of sky and trees were beautiful, but there was a memory round it. When Mother was a girl, a large garden-party was being held at Reskadinnick and the guests were having tea, playing croquet, and strolling about on the front lawn, while the boys and girls were helping to entertain them. The youngest child, a little chap of four

*Summer Afternoon Tea, by Thomas Barrett*

named Nicholas, had been given a piece of cake and had wandered down by himself into the side garden to play. After a while one of the guests noticed the beauty of the pond among the trees and walked down towards it. To his horror he found little Nicholas in the pond, into which apparently he had fallen, and either choked by a mouthful of cake, or unheard in the general talk, he had been drowned beyond hope of resuscitation.

'But what did they all do?' I used to ask Mother when she told me this story. I suppose methods of reviving were unknown, for nothing could she remember except the anguish and self-reproaches of her mother. How one weaves fancies round those who never grow up, and what a real immortality they have! I have thought my Uncle Nicholas would have been the best of all, and grieved for him out of all proportion.

Another pond was of considerable size, occupying the whole of the end of the mowey. Here we let ourselves go. The boys made a raft of two stout planks, and by means of broomsticks were able to navigate the whole pond. A high hedge separated it from the field beyond, but here and there was a foothold on the bank where one could land. Each of these landing-places had some far-flung name – the Cape, Straits Settlements, Yokohama, and so on. One day we enticed the cook up into the mowey 'for a sail'. She stepped cautiously on board (*le mot juste*), and before she could retreat Charles pushed off, and after a passage of peril and protest landed her at Madras. She was glad to feel the shore, but before she knew where she was Charles had put to sea again, leaving poor Temperance marooned. We other mariners in the home port shouted with joy, little considering that the family dinner was at stake. After raising the welkin to no effect, Temperance determined to try for an overland passage, and finally tore and scratched her way through the hedge into the lane. She was too devoted to the 'young gentlemen' to tell the grown-ups, and accounted for her scratches and the lateness of dinner in a way that would have satisfied Scotland Yard.

Many a time when the boys were off on some excursion of their own, far afield, and Beatrice was absorbed in domestic or social duties, Mina and I were left to ourselves. We had trained the grown-ups not to worry if we were late coming home. Tony was apt, however, to get fidgety if we did not turn up at dusk. 'Oh, my dears,' she would say, 'I was getting so hurried. I was afraid one of you had gone "over cliff."' 'Hurried' in Cornwall means 'anxious'; hence the saying: 'There was once an old woman who died in a hurry.' A tale was current about two little boys who went to the cliffs, one fell over, and the other was too paralysed with fright to go home until nightfall. This incident would seize Tony's imagination if any of us was late.

Apart, then, from a decently early return, nothing was expected of us. The authorities could rely on us to look after our own food-supply. I suppose no better education could be given two children than this freedom of the farm and countryside, and some of the happiest days of my life were spent with Mina, wandering about as chance directed. The grounds were so large that we were continually discovering some copse or hidden path or plantation that even Mina had not observed before. As a London child my ignorance about trees, poultry, and animals was complete, and all their ways were astounding. Warm eggs, eggs in the act of being laid, warm, foaming milk, a newly-born calf able to walk at once, absurd little chicks . . . and Mina explained everything to me. The mill was a never-failing show-piece: we saw how the water managed to turn the wheel; we liked the jolly clack-clack of the works, and to bury our arms in the grain as it poured out of a wooden shoot. Another star place to visit was the forge. The old blacksmith generally had something going on. Bible miracles paled for me beside the incredible way in which he twisted a piece of red-hot iron just as his whim directed.

It was in the lane by the smithy that Mina and I had our one and only quarrel. I have no recollection of what it was about, but I was more blindly furious than at any other time in my life. I stammered out, 'You are a carcass.' I had no idea what the word meant, but it seemed to satisfy me and certainly roused Mina. We agreed to fight it out, and asked the blacksmith to see fair play. Mina was a little older and heavier than I was, but I hadn't had four brothers for nothing, and knew some bits of the noble art. Mina was soon running indoors, calling heaven to witness her wounds. Tony appeared, looked at the 'bruises', declared them to be only dirt, and to Mina's intense chagrin washed them off. I was then rather sorry for her, apologized handsomely for my dreadful word, and all was well again.

Sometimes I would go forth quite alone, on some little errand for Tony, who said that a stranger from 'London town' would be impressive and entertaining to the numerous cottagers whom she befriended. I think that it was myself that was the more impressed usually. For instance, I was sent off to one of those cottages that have no privacy at all. I entered straight from the road, through the open door, into the living-room, and shall never forget the scene. Mrs Polglaze, a cripple, was perched on a high chair in one corner of the tiny space. Seated on a couple of benches opposite her were seven or eight little children, mumbling aloud together, and laboriously pointing their fingers along what I supposed must be books. So black were these with use that no one could possibly read them, and the children must have been chanting from memory. Making my way through to Mrs Polglaze I delivered Tony's pasties and fruit and butter, and was uncomfortable at her extreme gratitude. I returned to Tony full of questions.

'Yes, dear,' said she, ''tis a real school. Poor old Mrs Polglaze gets a penny a week for each child she takes.'

'But does she live on that?' I asked.

'Well, not entirely,' replied Tony, pushing off to her work.

Another task she gave me was more formidable. One of our numberless family cousins was an old lady of strong Wesleyan convictions, who lived in a large house in the town. She had expressed a wish to see Cousin Mary's little girl. Consequently I was made tidy and despatched. Mina stood by and darkly suggested that Cousin Jane would be certain to try to convert me. But Tony encouraged me by saying that I need not stay more than ten minutes, and 'You can go in on these', she added, giving me a bunch of fine geranium-blooms.

All went as scheduled. I entered brightly with the flowers, answered all the questions as to dear mamma's health, how the boys were doing at school, how long my holidays were to last, and generally kept my end up so well that I clean forgot any danger from religion. I had my trump card to get out on – that they would be getting hurried at home if I were late for dinner – and rose from my chair with easy confidence. Alas! Cousin Jane rose too, spread herself majestically between me and the door, raised her hand, and said,

'I trust, my dear child, that you have decided for the Lord?'

Now I had gathered from the boys that any one who is mad or drunk or peculiar in any way must be humoured. So with all the glowing enthusiasm I could muster I replied,

'Oh, *yes*, Cousin Jane!'

Seeing her look of extreme pleasure, I sought to complete my stroke, and added, 'Ra*ther!*'

At this she was so astonished that she was literally struck dumb, fell back a pace, and allowed me to slip past her, through the door, and out to freedom.

For one period every year there was a surfeit of out-door work for all. At harvest-time the whole place far and wide became a tornado of doings. Tony was anchored to the kitchen, producing portable food for the men in the fields and for us children. There was a great brewing of 'herby beer', which I once tasted because Edgar said it was good. Jars of this horrible liquor and of cider were everywhere available. The boys were all in two places at once. Uncle Joe was riding about on his horse, telling every one that this glorious spell of fine weather must be made the most of, for it surely couldn't last. And how we did work! There were no cutting-machines in those days, let alone binders. When I pass a harvest-field today I think how dull it seems. Yet how thankful Uncle Joe was when he was able to hire a machine for lifting the corn on to the rick.

Even I, the youngest of the crew, was able to do my bit, and I became quite an expert at binding, but could never equal the rate of the boys, who raced one another along the rows. Dinner-time was jolly. Not minding the heat we sat under one of the newly built corn-cocks, and devoured our pasties and cider. Then to work again, with no thought of anything so effeminate as tea, until dusk, when we returned to supper, weary and dirty, and went to bed early so as to be ready for the next day's work.

*Children of the Artist at St Michael's Mount, by Albert Goodwin*

One day of my childhood was completely lost, and a glorious sunny day at that. Very rarely, for it was an expensive treat, the whole family, grown-ups and children, would go off to some distance for a long day. Sometimes it would be Penzance and the Land's End, sometimes the Lizard, sometimes Falmouth. It was usual to hire two long wagonettes, lunch at an hotel, and be free of the trouble of a picnic. Now a particularly favourite spot for such an expedition was Prussia Cove, which was full of possibilities, and more homely than the show places. There were little fishing-vessels in which we could have a sail. Shells of a rare and beautiful kind were to be found on the beach. Bathing was safe in the deep pools, and there were endless bits that we could sketch. The inn had once been the headquarters of a famous old smuggler called the King of Prussia, and they could show you the false walls behind which he used to stow his kegs of brandy.

Well, one day we all set out for this desired haven, plotting during the long drive the special schemes that each had in mind. A big spread was to be provided for midday in the inn, and our only duty was to get up an appetite.

Arrived, my one and only thought was the sea. I ran on to a rock and promptly fell headlong into a pool.

'Oh, that's all right, darling,' said Tony. 'Come into the inn and we'll pop you into bed while we spread your clothes round the kitchen fire. They won't take above ten minutes or so.'

I fell fast asleep, and never woke until they were all getting ready to go home. I could have borne the misery of disappointment better if they hadn't said that they thought the sleep would do me good. As if one went to Prussia Cove for one's good!

*A 'Fan and Japonica' Chamber Set*

# 10

# INDOOR DOINGS

CORNISH people are nearly amphibious. Their peculiar mist of fine rain surrounds you in such a way that an umbrella is useless. Both this mist and slight showers are hardly regarded. But a steady downpour will occasionally keep you in if there is no pressing need to go out. On a really wet day, therefore, we children had to amuse ourselves indoors.

Although Reskadinnick was intricate and rambling enough to satisfy any child, it had a nucleus or nerve-centre round which the whole life of the place seemed to revolve. It was called the 'front kitchen', but had nothing of a kitchen about it. It had been the main living-room of the original old farmhouse, but now served no definite purpose at all. Like some large-hearted friend it had no absorbing worries of its own, and was always empty and free for anything you wanted. Nowhere else have I come across a large room set aside for no purpose, and yet used continually. The dining- and drawing-rooms were solemnly devoted to Sundays and visitors; but the 'front kitchen' was far more dignified than either, in its homely aura of quiet.

Along one side of this room ran a row of casement windows, provided by nature with a long window-seat. This formed a perfect hiding-place if you stretched your length and kept your head down, because a colossal table of snow-white wood, hard as iron, was placed close alongside the window. The only other furniture consisted of a high-backed settle, a chair or two, and a grandfather's clock in a recess. At one end was the fireplace, with a high mantelpiece, holding two shapeless china animals, probably cats, always staring, reminding Mother of the Cornishman who said his wife was 'no better than a cloamen cat'. The floor was paved with flagstones, never sanded as the ordinary kitchen was, and uncumbered by rug or carpet.

Here were held all family councils of moment, indignation meetings, and breaking of sad news. Here came Uncle Bill after he had written an important letter, to read it aloud, not to all the grown-ups together, but to each one in turn, to receive their admiration and slight improvements in the wording.

For one half-hour every day Tony would come here to 'do the milk'. The bulk of the dairy produce was sold to the cottages scattered over the downs, and for this purpose a stolid widow, named Mrs Veal, trundled round a two-wheeled barrow holding a big container with tap attached. Very slowly she laboured up hill and down dale, without ever speaking a word apparently. Nothing could ruffle her, and goodness knows we tried hard enough. On her return Tony would take a seat at the great white table and spread out her business paraphernalia, consisting of a slate, a little account-book with pencil attached, and a kind of missionary box. I often slipped into the window-seat to listen to the rare sound of Mrs Veal's voice, and marvel at her feats of memory. The ritual never varied: Tony read from her book the first name, thus: 'Mrs Bray,' and Mrs Veal would say, ''Aporth and paid for et,' laying down a halfpenny on the table. Tony put this into the box, made an entry on the slate, and went on to the next name – Mrs Pendray. Then Mrs Veal: ''Aporth and dedn't pay for et.' Another entry and another name. No one ever seemed to have more than a 'aporth, but many 'Dedn't 'ave any'. Watching this I hardly wondered that Mrs Veal never indulged in idle chat, while her memory was functioning.

Once a week the big table was used for folding and ironing the huge family wash. For this purpose the irons were put in the fire till red hot and then slipped into brightly polished steel boxes with wooden handles – click, click they went over the enormous sheets and tablecloths. One day when Barnholt was tiny he insisted on walking on the table all in the midst of the operations. 'Heave 'e down, Miss Tony,' suggested one of the servants. 'No heave 'e down,' cried Barnholt, and heaved down he was not.

Apart from these domestic ceremonies the table was always available for anything that required elbow-room, such as wetting, stretching, and pasting on to boards the large sheets of drawing-paper that mother, Beatrice, and Charles used for their water-colour sketches.

Such a room positively called for theatricals, and not content with mere charades we once attempted a real play, a full-blooded melodrama, whose only light relief was the unintended. Charles and Beatrice produced it, and we underlings just did as we were told. Mina was pretty and made a fine heroine, but refused to sing in public. The operatic air that was essential for the piece had to be sung by Beatrice behind a screen, while Mina kept opening and shutting her mouth. Beatrice was the queen mother, Charles the heartless villain, and Edgar the hero. He had to look brave and say almost nothing. In fact he had but one speech: 'Draw your sword at once, Sir, and do not chatter.'

*Domestic Lesson, by Arthur Cooke*

This came at the crisis before the duel, but Edgar, who was quite word-perfect in it, and was tired of being the strong, silent man, always burst out with it before the time.

Rehearsals went on all day, and whenever the rain stopped we would run out and go over separate bits 'obscenely and courageously' in the garden. Old wardrobes and chests were ransacked for our dressings-up, and there was much competition for a blue quilted petticoat, a many-coloured silk shawl that mother had brought from Spain, and a black velvet cape lined with crimson. I say rehearsals, because the play never reached fruition. Not only did Charles and Beatrice come to continual loggerheads over the details, but the weather improved on us to such an extent that outside distractions were too strong for the team to be kept together.

However, as the dressing-up was the chief attraction, this we could do at any time for less ambitious acting. Getting away from the boys one afternoon, we plotted to take them in. Beatrice and Mina laid themselves out to dress me up as a nun. My forehead, ears, and throat were swathed in a towel (how hot I was!), a black kerchief was drooped over my head, and a big black cloak pinned all round me. Then, watching my opportunity, I staggered out among the trees a little way down the drive, and thence approached the front door and knocked. This door was not often used except by strangers, and I had to wait till the housemaid had arranged herself to answer it. I had prepared a humble voice, and begged to see the lady of the house for a minute. I was then ushered obsequiously into the drawing-room. Choosing a seat with my back to the light I awaited my rather severe Aunt Knight. Thankful that it was not Tony, who would have spotted me, I began a most urgent appeal for a Home for Incurables. Now this was the kind of thing Aunt Knight liked, and she became quite emotional and full of inquiries. I worked myself up in describing a bad case, and she left the room to fetch a donation. At the door I heard her say, 'Do go in and speak to her a moment, Tom, it all seems very sad,' and who should come in but my brother, all politeness. I now pitched my tale a little higher, describing the harrowing scene when a patient was told that he was incurable, and should not we, who enjoyed such robust health, &c. I had not expected to encounter my eldest brother, who was only on a short visit and reckoned almost a grown-up, so what was my delight when I saw him putting his hand in his pocket as he murmured sympathetic dear-me's. When once I had grabbed his half-crown, I unveiled, and when Aunt Knight returned with her contribution she found us both in unseemly laughter.

Another time we all combined to disguise Charles as a distant cousin, a lady from the Cape, impersonating some one actually possible with a name that would 'go down'. Beatrice provided a dress and a flowing hat, and a pair of glasses made the get-up complete. When 'Miss Symons' had been ushered into the drawing-room, my aunts hurriedly improved their toilet, ordered tea to be laid in the dining-room, and swept in all graciousness of welcome. Mother never bothered to alter her attire for any one, but was equally taken in. Charles poured forth an endless flow of patter about the flora and fauna of South Africa, the beauties and dangers of the voyage, the impertinence of his steward, and so on, answering all inquiries with careful accuracy (for we had prepared a few to ask him). All went swimmingly, and we were well through tea when Barnholt began to splutter, and the game was up.

Not even the wettest day could keep us confined to the house itself for long. We would make a dash across the yards and over the lane to the barn, and sit reading there with a lapful of apples. Once we found the barn a foot deep in grain, and immediately began to swim in it, pretending to be Midas swimming in gold. Unfortunately we spoke of our swimming feats at the dinner-table and were forbidden in horrified tones to do it again. It seemed that it was not good for the wheat.

A still pleasanter city of refuge was the granary, a large loft stretching over the whole length of the stables. Its main attraction was the spice of danger in reaching it, as well as the feeling of security from detection when we were up. The ladder to it from the stables was not always in place, and when we had fixed it up it was always shaky. After mounting this ladder we had a nasty scramble through the trap-door at the top. Once up we could race to and fro to our hearts' content, and watch all the comings and goings in the yard, feeling superior to every one, even that horrible turkey-cock.

The boys were fond of rummaging in the Office. Here were a high desk and a chest, both containing documents, letters, plans of mines, maps, and account-books. They once unearthed some black stamps, many of which were valuable, being some of the earliest penny stamps ever issued.

When all else failed we fell back on drawing and painting in the front kitchen. I can remember no dull hour at Reskadinnick. And however dreadful the mess we made, Tony would always say: 'Where there is no ox the stall is clean.' As a child I thought this a funny remark, but now it seems quite otherwise.

*An Ivory China Lamp*

*The Cherry Pickers, by Berthe Morisot*

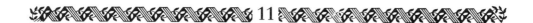 

# 11

# A FAMILY CLUB

L EAVING Cornwall was always a misery. Every accompaniment of it was miserable. We had to get up in the dark, choke down some breakfast, say good-bye to the cats, hope the station fly wouldn't come, wait on the lonely station platform for the fatal appearance of the train, scramble into any carriage, and worst of all wrench ourselves from Tony. Sometimes she would go as far as Truro with us, but that made the parting more prolonged and definitely worse.

However, spirits soon rose, for compensations became more weighty as the journey went on. Chief among these was the looking forward to seeing my father again, who was never able to spare more than a few days for a Cornish visit. We had heaps to tell him, and liked to show off our Cornish accent and turns of speech. For some time after our return we would say, 'Where's he to?' instead of the English, 'Where is he?' and 'Going out are you?' instead of 'Are you going out?' Tom had a theory that this method of putting the important word first came from our having been descended from the Romans. Our family name of Vivian was certainly of Roman origin. Some energetic member had the matter traced by experts, who 'discovered' to our immense delight that we were descended from the Roman centurion who jumped into the water crying, 'Desilite, milites!' To our fancy this brave invader fell in love with a Cornish maiden, and our lively family was the result, revelling in the motto: 'Dum vivimus vivamus'.

The name Vivian came in useful on our return journey, for our luggage was all labelled with it. At Paddington in those days all bags and trunks were arranged on the arrival platform under the letters of the alphabet. To find your belongings all you had to do was to go to the right initial. Since few people's names began with 'V', our baggage was to be seen in lonely state. It seems to me a good plan, for friends could also meet you at the initial. There we would find my father with cab engaged and all ready for us.

None but an old Londoner can understand the curious attraction of the town. After the music of the words 'London only' at Reading, we gave ourselves up to the *nil admirari* spirit. The size and importance of the terminus might alarm a timid fellow passenger, but were nothing to us. The wet streets (for it invariably seemed to rain on our return), the reflections from the street-lamps and the shops, the utter indifference of everybody to us and our concerns — why was it fascinating even to a child? I suppose we took on that feeling of superiority to all the world, the idea of finality, that London gives. No sign-posts to other towns are to be seen. Here's London. Here you are. We were almost of the same mind as the old Cornish farm-labourer who could not be made to believe that there was anything *beyond* London.

Mother's power of producing a spread on our return home was able to work at a distance, for my main recollection of coming into the house was a big meal laid ready on the dining-room table, and the excited talk of all our doings as we sat round it. My father and usually Tom as well had to be shown all our sketches, bits of Cornish stone and shells, and be told all our jokes and hairbreadth escapes. The grief at leaving Cornwall was definitely over.

A change came over our home life when Tom left Shrewsbury. His education, except for Latin and Greek, had to begin again, and he started preparing for a London degree. Dym taught him mathematics, for his ideas in that line were hardly better than mine. Although literature was almost part of the family furniture and not a 'subject' in those days, history had to be studied, for Shrewsbury had been aware of nothing later than the Roman Empire. French he read every day with Mother.

With all this being done at home, and Dym preparing for a mathematics scholarship at Cambridge, the study became more a work-room than a play-room, and some kind of order had to be maintained. Now whatever else Tom had failed to learn at Shrewsbury he had acquired the knack of ruling others, and by common consent he became a kind of Dictator. A general meeting was held, and he divulged a grand scheme for organizing our life in the study on democratic lines. A family club was formed, to be called 'The Library'. The set of rules drawn up was to be as binding as the Decalogue. Like the Decalogue they were ten in number and chiefly negative. 'Thou shalt not' was the tone, but they did not interfere with the liberty of the decently behaved.

Although Mother had nothing whatever to do with the affair, she must have been very glad of these rules, for they enabled the household to run smoothly without her having to harry, scold, or punish. Thus, in addition to regulations about work in the study, they forbade being late to breakfast (i.e. coming down after grace was said), going upstairs with boots on, omitting to brush your teeth, not hanging up coat and cap, and suchlike tiresome points for a

mother to watch.

You may wonder how the club managed to enforce its rules. We all had definite pocket-money once a week, except me. I merely levied money from my father whenever I wanted some. Tom's plan was that we should be fined a penny, twopence, &c., up to sixpence, according to a definite scale of charges every time we broke a rule. He bought an account-book, assigned a page to each of us, and reckoned up how much each owed at the end of the week.

Still you may wonder how the payment of the fines was enforced. It was quite simple – no payment, no entry to the study. Since the study was the heart of our home, to be shut out of it was misery. Only once was there a failure to pay up. Barnholt was not recalcitrant, but bankrupt. I shall never forget the two days that he was shut out, wandering disconsolately about the house, doing his hateful lessons on the stairs. Mother was wrung with pity, and so indeed were all of us, but we dared not interfere with discipline by subsidizing him. However, I had private means, could stand it no longer, and advanced him something . . . and Tom had the sense to make no ugly inquiries.

Tom soon found what he had no doubt hoped – that we had quite a nice little sum of money. He then unfolded his larger plan: the club was to be a real library. The shelves that had been decorated with childish fancies were cleared and made ready for books, and the first outlay was to be an additional bookcase that Charles had seen in Upper Street second hand. The books themselves made quite a respectable show. Tom had brought a good many from Shrewsbury, one of which was actually a prize. Dym had plenty of prizes and a lot of mathematical books. One I took to be *Comic Sections* was very disappointing when I opened it. Charles and even Barnholt had gained a prize or two, and we all had several gift books. When we had levied some Scott and Dickens from the bookcase downstairs our shelves began to look businesslike.

Imagine our excitement when we found that soon after the bookcase had been bought we had enough money to buy a *new* book. The number of books suggested, the meetings we held, the time spent in discussing the various possibilites – it all seems beyond belief today, when books are so cheap. The die was cast at last. Our love of *Ungava* determined us to get another of Ballantyne's, and Tom was commissioned to buy *The Iron Horse*. I asked Charles what it would be about. 'It'll be something like the story of the wooden horse at Troy, I hope,' said he. Surely no book was ever read and re-read and talked over as that first new volume, although we went on to buy many more.

After a while we were in sufficient funds to take in some magazines. *Sunshine* and *Little Folks* for the younger ones, and *Cassell's Family Magazine* for us all. I can still remember the deep interest I took in a long serial story called 'March Winds and April Showers bring forth May Flowers'. To my great satisfaction it didn't turn out to be all about nature, but about a large family of boys and girls, who got into scrapes, quarrelled, and made it up again, and had various jolly adventures. One short story in my magazine was amusing enough for the boys to read. 'Don't let the Joneses know' described some children going to a party. They were in distress because they had only a donkey-cart to go in. The rich Joneses were their special dread. These rich people would roll up in their carriage and pair, and would laugh if they heard about the donkey. 'Whatever you do, don't let the Joneses know' — that was the order of the day. Scheming by various delays to arrive late so as to slip in unobserved, they drew up at the precise moment that the Joneses had hit upon. Steeling themselves for the worst, they were astonished to find all the Joneses crowding round their cart, not with jeers, but with delighted admiration. 'How lovely! Look! A real donkey! And Harry driving it himself!' By this time the other guests had run out to look, and all were exclaiming, 'Oh, how we wish we had a donkey!' In fact they and their donkey were the main topic of talk and source of envy all the evening.

Mother specially liked this story, for it illustrated her oft-repeated injunction that for comfort and success in life one must never suppose that any other people whatsoever are one's social superiors, 'because,' she added succinctly, 'they aren't'.

*Cassell's Magazine* provided stronger meat, far more substantial than we get in the average magazine today. It had to last us a month, and I think every word of it found some reader in the family. When we had all read the portion of the serial story, and very definitely not before, we discussed endlessly at tea-time how the characters would turn out and who would marry whom. With so little new reading-matter to distract us we were able to carry all the details in our head until the next issue. The plot seems simple as I look back on it: a girl was engaged to a man whom duty bade her marry, while she was really in love with another. No one in those stories was ever actually married to the wrong man. To me the triangle seemed insoluble, and I was all prepared for a broken heart and tears. But Charles announced one day that the first young man would die, and all would be well. 'How do you know?' we asked him. 'I noticed him cough in the second chapter.'

*The Night Before the Exam, by Leonid Pasternak*

Charles broke our rule of never discussing a book's plot with one still reading it, when he saw me one day deep in *A Journey to the Interior of the Earth*. 'Have you come to where they all die?' said he. I read on, expecting the worst on every page, until the end showed them all alive and well. I went to Charles in no little heat. 'Well,' said he, 'I never said they all died, I only asked you if you had come to it. And if you weren't a little silly you would know that they couldn't have *all* died, or who was left to tell the story?'

Wedding-bells were the usual end to our stories, of which *The Heir of Redclyffe* was a fair sample. Needless to say I had no notion of any difficulties after the bells had pealed. I took it for granted that husbands and wives were as happy as my own parents, with the exception of Aunt Bessie who grumbled at nothing, and Aunt Lizzie's husband who got drunk and threw things at her, a surely unusual case. *Vanity Fair* I read without the faintest suspicion of the intent of the note in the bouquet, or of Rawdon's reason for knocking down Lord Steyne. I thoroughly enjoyed that scene, although it seemed quite uncalled for.

One winter evening I was sitting over the fire engrossed in *Jane Eyre*, and had just got to where Grace Poole seems to be more than meets the eye, when Charles appealed to Mother to take the book from me as being not very proper.

She looked up, surprised, and then said, 'Oh, ah, yes, perhaps she had better not read it,' and took the book from me as suggested. Charles only meant it in fun, and was sorry that Mother had taken it seriously, but the deed was done.

As a make-weight to our lighter magazines we took in the *Nineteenth Century*, and the elder boys read some of the articles. I struggled through one by Gladstone, in order to be able to say I had, but honestly I understood no single sentence. We were brought up in the belief that Gladstone was semi-divine, and to read an article by him ranked with reading the Bible. However, Tom introduced a wholesome note of doubt on this point, and also on the absolute worshipfulness of Queen Victoria.

'I think she has had a pretty easy time of it,' said he, startling the tea-table, after one of Mother's tributes to our beloved Queen.

'Oh, no!' cried Mother, 'she has walked on the edge of a sword.' Thereafter I always pictured the Queen engaged in this absurd feat. I had been taken to see her once as she drove along Essex Road, and my memory of her made the idea of her walking on a sword merely funny. She was a shadowy figure to most people, but every one loved the Prince of Wales. He took a hansom once, and next thing you knew he might be in an omnibus. I asked Mother what she would do if the Prince were to drop in to see us. 'I should offer him a little whisky and water,' was her immediate reply.

In the summer of 1877 Tom started a new idea. Not content with our magazines, he suggested that we should make one of our own. Of course we took up the idea with fervour, and meetings were held to decide the paper to be used, the size of the page, the material and colour of the cover. Its name was *The Bee*, because it was to go from flower to flower collecting honey for its readers, as Tom explained in a poem on the first page. He, of course, was the Editor, Dym the science special correspondent, Charles 'our artist' and provider of light fiction. But there was very little light about the publication, in which everything was expressed as solemnly as possible.

We had no reproducing machine, so that it all had to be written in manuscript. In order to preserve uniformity of appearance Tom copied it all himself. He sat at one end of the study table and it was a point of honour not to look. Charles did a water-colour frontispiece for each number, one of Canonbury Tower, another of St Paul's from Merchant Taylors' School playground, and a large number of pen-and-ink illustrations. I was allowed to do some little tail-pieces.

Tom wrote heavy articles in the style of the *Nineteenth Century*, on such subjects as 'The effect on Poetry of Science', 'The Penge Case', and 'The Ritualists'. Charles described Wagner's *Lohengrin*, and provided a serial story. Dym wrote on Voltaic Electricity, with diagrams of test-tubes and things, and on the Russo-Turkish Relations. I managed an account of a picnic in Cornwall, and a poem on my cat. I can remember pacing up and down my bedroom in torture of composition for my last line, which was rung out at last with more truth than rhythm. The final stanza ran thus:

> *Of a very bad cough*
> > *Poor Pinky died,*
> *But I must now finish off,*
> > *Which to do I've often tried.*

Tom kept to himself that in the original her fatal disease was spelt 'coff'.

Tom got blood out of a stone, for he actually extracted a contribution from Barnholt. There was a symposium in the November issue on 'Flogging at School', on which each expressed his opinion. Barnholt produced no fewer than twenty-two lines on the subject. His opening remark was arresting: 'Flogging is a very good substitute for boys who will not work.' The burden of his article was that any punishment was better than endless detentions.

Each number of *The Bee* was placed by my father's side at the breakfast-table, that he might have the virgin glance. His genuine admiration and pride were ample reward for all our trouble. It was then passed round the family to be read in turn, and such care did we take of the five numbers we produced that they are still as clean today as when they left Tom's hands, and the fifty years and more have hardly faded the ink. I am still fond of poring over them, all except Barnholt's little essay, which I find too much of a human document . . . so many hours of his short life to have been spent in senseless detention!

*Canonbury Tower, drawn by Charles for THE BEE*

# 12

# A LAST CHRISTMAS

THE jolliest winter of our childhood was in 1878. We had only given up making our magazine because real work was too pressing. Tom was at the last phase for his B.A. and Dym was in full hopes of his Cambridge scholarship. Charles had left school in order to give his whole time to his water-colour painting. Most of his days were spent in town, copying the technique of David Cox, Turner, and Muller, and we all looked forward to seeing what he brought home every evening. He had sold so many of his own original sketches that he confidently hoped to make his living in that way.

Of the four boys Barnholt was perhaps the happiest. Released at last from his eternal 'detentions', he had been taken from school and placed in a shipping office, with the prospect of next year fulfilling the dream of his life by going to sea. As Mother had predicted, he was the first of us to earn his living, to have a real salary, to be a 'man of means'. I fancy that he had suffered a good deal from having to wear the other boys' left-offs, for the first thing he did was to buy quite quietly a new suit. I can see him now as he walked into breakfast in it. It was a grey tweed, bristling with newness, and we were all full of admiration as he went off with my father 'to the City', while Mother proudly demanded to know what she had told us.

And I too was happy in the first flush of my school-days, involving important 'homework' at the study table. At my October birthday the family came out strong: Tom bought a papier-mâché pencil-box that shut firmly and had Chinese figures doing something on the lid. Inside were three compartments. In the longest of these Charles put five new lead pencils (ranging from HH to BB). In the middle-sized division Dym put a penknife, and in the smallest division Barnholt put a piece of soft india-rubber. Mother gave me a pair of scissors to be entirely my own, and my father brought me home the loveliest umbrella ever designed. It was of dark blue silk, and had a carved ivory handle. He must have given a lot for it, and I could never bring myself to use it. I carried it to school every day firmly grasped round the middle, but never opened it. When I was driven, one day much later, by a sudden shower to

*A Hansom Cab Stand, by P. Stahl*

loosen the elastic band and spring it open, what was my dismay to find the silk in shreds where my hand had worn it.

The pencil-box was the envy of my school-fellows. The boys were greatly tickled at the way in which I assigned a special pencil for use in the various subjects – a history pencil, a geography pencil, and so on. 'I say, Molly, lend us your Scripture pencil,' Dym would say, for he knew that was an H, and good for his geometry figures. They all took an amused interest in my lessons and my 'little friends', as they called my school-fellows. My father, too, used to ask what I was doing, and one day, by way of reply, I inflicted on him the recitation of a whole poem about Mary Queen of Scots. This began:

*I looked far back into other years, and lo, in bright array.*

I haven't the faintest notion now of what I saw in bright array, but the closing lines have stuck in my memory. They refer to the blood of the queen, and run thus:

*The noblest of the Stuart race, the fairest Earth hath seen,*
*Lapped by a dog! Go, think of it, in silence and alone,*
*Then weigh against a grain of sand the glories of a throne.*

Neither I nor my father thought of carrying out these instructions, but he gave me sixpence and said it was very good.

He used to help me with my sums, going very slowly with his explanations and telling me about things they did 'in the City'. He taught me how to write quickly by never taking off my pen in the middle of a word, and gave me 'transubstantiation' to practise on. I aimed at copying his handwriting, which I still think the best I have ever seen. . . .

My ideas about the City were confused. Sunday showed me a peaceful wilderness, where one walked in the middle of the road. Barnholt's accounts were of crowds of people, and the following scrap of conversation between Father and Mother didn't help matters.

'Seen any one in the City today, Tom dear?'

'Not a soul, except old Herring.'

I pictured a herring suspended somewhere on a string across the street. Mother didn't seem in the least surprised at the lack of population.

To us one November evening there came a casual knock at the door, and who should walk in but Tony. Better than the comfort of being met at the station was the joy to her of giving us all such a surprise. As we crowded round her she explained that she had just 'slipped away' to spend a week or two with us. A telegram would seem to have been the natural thing to send, but in those days telegrams were nearly always reserved for disasters, so that the yellow envelope in itself was a shock, and care was taken that the person to whom it was delivered should be seated ready for the worst. Tony laughingly said she was sure of a welcome, and knew that Mother could always throw up a bed.

She then disclosed that she had not come alone, but was to be shortly followed by a barrel of apples and a young pig, coming on by goods train. The barrel was delivered first and was installed in the china-closet near the front door, and we had full permission to help ourselves whenever we liked. The young pig, technically known as a 'porker', arrived wrapped in canvas on the carrier's shoulder, and was laid on the kitchen table ready for cutting up. It seemed to involve the whole household in feverish activity for days. There was glory for the servants, since all regular work was pushed aside in the effort to find big earthenware pans, to fetch in saltpetre and treacle, and clean up. The boys were summoned to help cut the big joints, and to pack up some of them to be sent to relations. I helped chop up the small meat ready for Mother and Tony to make into sausages and pork pies.

Naturally Tony wanted to see the shops, and as soon as the Christmas holidays began I was allowed to go with her and Mother to the West End. Tony was all for taking hansoms. As she pointed out, a bus can be taken any day – a holiday was a holiday, and she didn't believe in doing things by halves. She argued that it is the regular expenses that one should worry about, not the occasional. So she took hansoms right and left, and I can still recall the luxurious feeling of snuggling down in a hansom between her and Mother, to be wafted exactly where we wanted to go. I could just see the toss of the horse's head and could hear the klip-klop of his hoofs and the cheerful jingle of his bells. It is amusing to reflect now that the bells on a hansom were put there as a warning to pedestrians to get out of the way of such swift vehicles. Those were the days when a man with a red flag used to walk in front of a steam-roller. I wonder what Tony would say to the traffic in Piccadilly today. On one of her later visits to London I took her on the top of a bus, to see some of the life of the town. As I called her attention to this and that, she said, 'Don't ask me to look, dear. If I take my eye off the driver he will surely run into something.'

What she suffered in a hansom I can't imagine, for she had no control over the driving, even with her eye. But in 1878 the traffic was laughably simple, and the only likelihood of an accident was the slipping of a horse on a wet road. Even then the driver from his high seat could usually pull the horse to his feet again. But Mother would never let the glass window in front be used, however hard it might rain, because a sudden fall of the horse might easily throw us headlong through the glass.

A morning's shopping was all we could manage for one day, for, strange as it seems now, the big shops had no restaurants, no rest-rooms, no conveniences for toilet, however dire one's need. The first tea-shop was opened at London Bridge, out of sheer pity for lady customers!

Much energy was spent in restraining Tony from buying too many presents, for the shops were so enticing. We found it safer to take her for expeditions to Epping, Hadley Woods, and Kew. One day I was allowed as a great treat to take her up to Hampstead Heath all by myself. Inducing her to tell me stories, I distracted her attention (and apparently my own) from the route we were following. At a strategic point I stopped suddenly, looked bewildered, and declared that I had lost the way. In reality I had led her in and out among short lanes and little paths, to and fro, and was all the time within easy distance of the station. At first I enjoyed seeing how 'hurried' she became, but when she talked of looking for a policeman, finding a post office, and telegraphing to Mother, I thought it was time to discover the station, and with a bright 'Here it is after all!' ushered her into the booking-office.

As Christmas drew nearer we had several evening gatherings, not formal enough to call parties, for the boys and their friends. Charles called them 'Robin Adair' parties, because a girl we knew used to trill forth this song on the slightest pressure. Aunt Polly would always oblige with 'Tell them they need not come wooing to me', occasioning many ribald remarks from the boys. Another song that became familiar was 'She wore a wreath of roses'. No one knew why she had this headgear, and when the poor fellow saw her again she had changed it. 'Methinks,' he sang, 'I see her now, with a wreath of orange-blossoms upon her marble brow.' One evening my father was begged to sing a song, and what was our astonishment when he stood out on the hearth-rug and without any accompaniment gave forth 'The Bells of Aberdovey', in glorious rich tones. Seeing every one's pleasure no doubt heartened him on, and his careless unconcern enabled him to get the full effect of the lovely Welsh words.

One of Tony's presents was a magic lantern, which she delivered before Christmas, so that the boys might practise it beforehand. Wonders are so thick today that no child can understand my thrill at the darkened study and the sight of coloured figures chasing one another in mid-air.

Everything combined to make this Christmas (the last we were to have all together) the best of all. Ambitious now with their acting, the boys attempted a real play – *Box and Cox*. Tom and Dym took the title-roles, and Charles that of Mrs Bouncer. Happily for me there was no heroine, and I could enjoy it all to the full. There was Dym cooking a chop over the study fire, and only leaving in the nick of time before Tom came in all hatted and overcoated, and there was Charles always in a dither. The whole thing was a success, loudly applauded by the grown-ups, including Tony and several others. A magic-lantern display followed, and then we all assembled downstairs for the presentation of Christmas gifts.

This was on a larger scale than ever before. The boys joined forces to give me *Aventures d'Alice au Pays des Merveilles*. They were proud of this book because the translation had been done by Henri Bué, the French master at Merchant Taylors'. My curiosity was to see how he had put into French 'Off with his head!' and I was amply satisfied with the funny way he rendered it.

Barnholt guessed rightly that I wanted a more frivolous note, so he added to my pile a mouse that would run along the floor when wound up. All other presents have slipped my memory, with the grand exception of those we children gave my father. We had each bought him a book, and my vividest memory of him is that jolly scene. There he sat, gazing at the pile of five books – too pleased to speak, too pleased to touch them.

The November of 1879 was cold and dark with fogs far worse than ever happen now. We used to look out to see torches being carried, and making ghastly glares in the deep yellow. One evening my father did not return. He had been run over and instantly killed. They did not dare to tell Mother. She went next day into the City to inquire, and was told by my uncle that Tom had been called away on business to Doncaster. And she waited somehow till two days had passed, when they came and broke the news. During the years that followed she used to sit in the dusk, in a chair facing the gate, as she had waited for Barnholt years before. I think she almost hoped that the past was only a nightmare, and that she would surely see my father coming up the garden path with his springy step, and would hear his familiar knock.

*London, Parliament with the Sun Breaking through Fog, by Claude Monet*

*The Duet*

# 13

# AN ORDINARY GIRL, 1881

*Your father, dear old chap, is always so anxious about you, and afraid of your
becoming an ordinary schoolgirl, with an ordinary schoolgirl's tricks and
mannerisms.*

THIS sentence is part of a letter from my mother to me in 1879, when at the age of twelve I was spending my summer holiday in Cornwall. The term 'old chap' was merely one of endearment, for he was only a little over forty, and to us children more like an elder brother than a father. He never worried us about our behaviour, so that any hint he let drop was the more significant. And when a few weeks later in that same year he met with a fatal accident, it was natural for us to treasure everything that we remembered about him. The particular hint quoted above was occasioned by a letter I had written home with several postscripts and facetious turns of phrase. I knew quite well that what he meant by 'ordinary' was the silly attempt to be extraordinary, and that he wanted me to be as simple and straightforward as possible. The same idea had been rubbed in by my four elder brothers, with less delicacy. So, paradoxically, I tried to carry out the wishes of these my household gods by being as ordinary and as little conspicuous as I could, suppressing a child's desire to shine by using grand words and witticisms – all that the boys summed up in the dreaded phrase 'trying to be funny'.

My mother's ideas for me gave a healthy make-weight. She was for encouraging any scrap of originality in anybody at any time, and allowed me to 'run free' physically and mentally. She had no idea of keeping her only girl tied to her apron-strings, and from childhood I used to go out alone in our London suburb of Canonbury, for a run with my hoop or to do a little private shopping, and once even went to Cornwall by myself. Her precepts were extremely few and consequently attended to. 'Never talk to any one in the street except to tell them the way.' To back this up, lurid stories were told me of children offered sweets by a 'kind lady', or taken for a ride in a gig by a 'kind gentleman', and never heard of again. The mystery of their fate was alluring, but deterrent enough. When a little older, I was warned, 'If out late, walk fast and look preoccupied, and no one will bother you.' Why I should be bothered I had no idea, but adopted the line of conduct without question.

⁜

But Mother had begun to think a bit, as mothers will, and when October brought my sixteenth birthday she took me seriously into the dining-room and began thus:

'Listen, dear. Now that the boys will soon be all scattered at their various work we shan't need such a big house as this. And we needn't be tied to London. Suppose you and I were to go and live together in a cottage down in Cornwall? Somewhere by the sea, such as St Ives or Marazion – within reach of Tony at Reskadinnick?'

She paused, giving a chance for these magic names to take effect, and then added: 'You could work at literature and read French with me. We could do lots of sketching. In fact we could do whatever we liked. You could have a horse and ride to all those parts of Cornwall that you've always wanted to see – Mevagissey, Zennor, Tintagel. Perhaps we might travel abroad, to Italy, Norway, Spain.'

'But how could we afford to – ' I broke in, knowing how limited were our means, but she stopped me with,

'I have already talked to the boys about the idea, and they have assured me that we shall always have enough to live on – they will see to that.'

Then, looking away from me out of the window for a few moments in silence, she turned and said in a dull, careless tone, 'Or – would you rather earn your own living?'

I hesitated. Rosy visions of Cornwall and its romantic villages, possession of a horse (always a passionate desire), the sea, Italy and Rome, floated in my imagination. It must have been a bit of my father's blood that made me say,

'It's awfully good of the boys to say that, and I know they mean it, but I would rather be independent.'

Mother smiled and admitted that the 'lady of leisure' idea had been the boys' and not hers. I know that she must have hoped for that decision; for it was habitual with her to load the dice in favour of the result she least wanted, for fear of influencing the choice.

In those few moments the current of my life was definitely set towards hard work and uncertainty, and although these two have been my constant companions, and several times I have been in very low water, never have I

*Sorrowful News, by F.D. Hardy*

regretted my choice.

The next point to consider was how the earning of a living was to be done. In those days it was not considered the thing for a girl to 'earn', although she might toy with a little work. Any other career than teaching was practically unknown. For me it would have to be teaching in a school, since the word 'governess' had become a grim joke in our family. During my last term at school one of the girls had told me that a friend of hers knew a girl who had actually become a B.A. We had both been awe-struck that a woman one might meet could attain such glory, but we neither of us connected this pinnacle with an ordinary teacher in a school. Indeed, I fancied that one just 'took up' teaching in the same casual way that I had taken a Sunday-school class last summer in Cornwall.

By the way, that bit of experience might well have given me pause. My cousin Lucy had been distracted by the vast number of children committed to her care on Sunday afternoons, and implored me to come and take a class. The section she assigned to me consisted of some forty children, aged from three to twelve, herded in a stale-smelling room, and supposed to be seated on long wooden forms. However, the only restriction to their jumping up or crawling about was the tightness with which they had been sewn into their Sunday clothes. Not even the death of Jezebel (the lesson appointed for the day) had any appeal, and my efforts to draw what moral I could from this story were continually interrupted by such remarks as 'Please, teacher, stop Tommy crawlin' on 'is best trowsies' and other intimate requests requiring immediate personal attention. Of course, truly Cornish, they wanted to know where I had come from, why I had my hair cut short like a boy's, and what I had paid to have it cut. I was foolish enough to admit that I had come from London. This started a new excitement, and I was asked if the pavements were really made of gold, and whether there were lions there. Seizing this last as a godsend, I abandoned Jezebel and spent the rest of the lesson in the Zoo.

I suppose it was the memory of this at the back of my mind that made me say to Mother that I felt a bit young to teach in a real school.

'Yes, exactly,' she replied, 'and it is only this morning that I've had a letter from Tony suggesting that you should go to the very best school that can be found, and that she will pay the fees, no matter how high.'

Tony was mother's favourite sister in Cornwall, an aunt who never knew how to do enough for us. She had been told of the birthday choice to be put before me, had guessed how I should decide it, and was determined that her present to me should consist in a proper preparation. 'I know what she will say,' ran the letter, 'so look sharp and find a good school.'

Now it chanced that as I used to go along Highbury New Park to my school I had frequently met a girl on her way to the station, carrying books and obviously going to school herself. After a while we used to smile on one another and then came to saying 'good morning,' and finally used to stop for a few moments' gossip.

'Where do you go to school?' was of course my first inquiry.

'The North London Collegiate, the biggest school in England, and the finest. You must have heard of it, and of its famous headmistress, Miss Buss?'

No, I hadn't, but I was not to be squashed, and she had to listen to my glowing description of our Prize-day.

'You call that grand!' she exclaimed. 'Why, who do you think gave away *our* prizes? The Princess of Wales!'

I had been duly impressed with this and with later information about the hundreds of girls, the examinations they were going in for, and the great assembly hall. I hadn't given much thought to these glories, but they came to my mind when we were wondering what school would be best for me. So I recounted to Mother all I could remember about this big school, whose name, 'The North London Collegiate', had remained in my mind, as well as its locality – Camden Town. I also recalled the name of the head, Miss Buss. Mother thought that she might venture a note to ask for particulars. A reply came at once to the effect that I might enter the school, provided that I pass the entrance examination, that I obeyed all the regulations, and that my fees were paid in advance.

'Entrance examination?' said I. 'Won't it do if you tell them I've passed the Senior Oxford?'

'Apparently not, dear, for I mentioned it in my note.' I felt that I was indeed up against something big. What would they expect for their entrance examination?

An afternoon was fixed for me to attend, and taking the train from Highbury to Camden Town I found my way to the school – a formidable-looking building. Seeing some steps labelled 'Pupils' Entrance' I went down them, told the first person I saw the reason of my appearance and was ushered into a room in the basement. Here I was provided with paper, pens, and ink, and various sets of questions which I could take in any order.

Keyed up as I was for something stiff, these papers seemed to me pifflingly easy. As for an explanation of the tides, I knew much more about them than the men of science do today, and drew beautiful diagrams to show how the water was piled up, in Biblical style, with no visible means of support. A blank map of Africa was to be filled in with 'all you know', and I was still busily inserting rivers and mountains, towns and capes, when all the papers were collected. I had floored them all, even the arithmetic, and sat back in a slightly supercilious mood. The very large and motherly official (addressed as Miss Begbie) who swam towards me looked a little surprised as she gathered up my stack of answers, and was almost deferential as she said,

'Now, dear, just make a buttonhole before you go.'

This was a quite unexpected blow. I confessed that I hadn't the faintest idea how to set about it, and thought that buttonholes just 'came'. Up went Miss Begbie's hands in shocked surprise.

'What! A girl of sixteen not know how to make a buttonhole!'

'Can't I come to the school then?' I asked in dismay.

'Well, possibly, dear. We shall see. But you must go home, learn to make a buttonhole, and come again this day week to make it.'

Mother was watching at the window for my return, and as she opened the door I exclaimed, 'I've failed.' How heartily she laughed when she heard of my disgrace. 'A buttonhole! Why, I'll teach you to make one in five minutes.' So indeed she did, and I practised the trick so assiduously all the week that even now I can make a buttonhole with the best. Meanwhile Mother made me a little case to hold needles, cotton, scissors, and thimble, to take with me, 'to look businesslike'. On the appointed day I appeared, was given a piece of calico, made my buttonhole, and went home. It seemed absurd to take the railway journey just for that, but it was a rule of the school that no girl should enter who couldn't make a buttonhole.

A few days later Mother received a notice that I had passed, and might enter the school in January.

*A Defiance Lockstitch Sewing Machine*

# 14

# UNDER LAW, 1883

AND now for my first day in the grand new school. I was as proud of my season-ticket from Highbury to Camden Town as any girl of later days with her latch-key. On it was inscribed 'with the privilege of alighting at intermediate stations'. This amused the boys, for the only intermediate station was Barnsbury, where no one ever went; Tom said it was only poets and railway-passengers who 'alighted'. With this talisman in my pocket I was able to pass the booking-office as though it didn't exist, and mutter 'season' in an off-hand manner at the barriers – a taste of life indeed.

As I walked up Camden Road I indulged in rosy dreams of all the brainy people I was about to meet. Mary Worley would have gone with me, but the new girls had been told to arrive an hour later than the rest. Consequently Prayers were over and the school was absorbed in the quietude of work, when some fifty of us new-comers were ushered into cloak-rooms and thence into a large theatre-shaped room, to be instructed in the ways of the school. A melancholy official began to read aloud a number of regulations. She had only read a few when she suddenly stopped, pointed at a girl in the middle of us, and exclaimed,

'Take off that locket, dear.' (By the way, I soon noticed that every remark to a girl was followed by the word 'dear'.)

I can see that poor girl now, very red in the face, fumbling with the chain of her locket. It seemed that there was a rule forbidding any unnecessary ornament. This didn't trouble me because Mother had kept me severely puritanical in this line, even reproving me once for wearing a ring out of a Christmas cracker. School uniforms were then unknown, so some restriction in dress was no doubt needed, but the lack of politeness to that poor girl gave me a shock.

A gracious welcome was certainly not the note of this preliminary harangue, the main object of which was obviously to chasten our spirits, in case we should think the place a free and easy affair like the régime of the despised private governesses or schools to which we had been accustomed. 'No nonsense here'

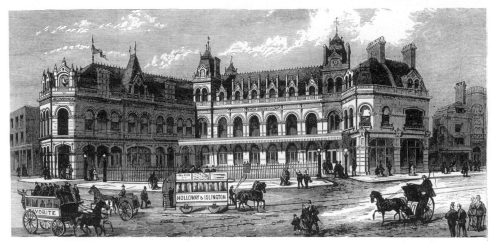

*Islington and Highbury Station*

was the key-note. It certainly had an imposing effect on me, and I was impatient to get to work, although a little dazed by the many instructions. At last we were dismissed, with orders to go to the various Forms to which we had previously been assigned by letter.

'Whereabouts is the Upper Fourth?' I asked.

'You must not speak without putting up your hand, dear.'

'Sorry', said I, and repeated my question with my hand hoisted.

'You should say "please" at the end of your question, dear.'

I tried again in proper style and was told,

'You will find the name of the Form on the door, dear.'

We dispersed in various directions, and presently I found myself alone, and quite lost. The passages were deserted. Through the glass door of each room I passed I saw serried ranks of girls at work. Nowhere could I find a room labelled 'Upper Fourth', although there were several other species of Fourth. Presently I caught sight of a little white-haired old woman, cap on head, and dressed in black rather the worse for wear. Some caretaker or cleaner or something, I thought, but she may possibly have noticed the names of the classrooms; I can but try. So I hailed her in a manner I thought appropriate.

'I say, am I going right for the Upper Fourth, do you happen to know?'

Glaring at me she exclaimed, 'Do you know who I am?'

'I haven't the faintest idea; I've only just come.'

'I am Miss Buss!' and standing back a pace she drew herself up to mark the effect on me. It was not at all what she expected, for I cheered up and said,

'Oh, then *you* are sure to know the way to the Upper Fourth, and I do so want to get there.'

At this suddenly her face changed, and with a little gay laugh she said, 'That way, child, down the stairs, the first door you come to at the foot. Run along with you.'

Thus oddly enough, it was in my first encounter with Miss Buss that I saw several different phases of her strange personality: her insignificance of stature and attire (*natura et arte*), her pomposity when she desired to impress, her kindly good temper, and her instantaneous and delighted recognition of any one who was quite at ease with her. These points didn't strike me at the moment, of course, but on recounting the incident to a seasoned schoolfellow afterwards I learnt that Miss Buss positively loved any one who was not afraid of her, who would look her in the eye and speak out.

At the moment I was far more intent on the Upper Fourth than on the headmistress. I was craving to see those wonderful girls, as low down in the school as the Fourth, to whom the Senior Oxford was a bagatelle.

Well, I found that Upper Fourth, and the very word gives me a mental shudder even now. After my dreams of cultured teachers and keen-brained girls — how humiliating was the drop! Any empty desk among some thirty others was pointed out to me, with a hurried 'Sit there, dear.' Something that seemed like geography was in progress, and the girls were being questioned round out of Cornwell's Geography, a text-book only too familiar to me. After an astonished taking in of the dreadful reality I relieved my feelings by a contemptuous remark to the girl in the adjoining desk. She placed a warning finger on her mouth, but was too late. The teacher had heard an unwarranted voice and beckoned me to her desk. Thrusting an open exercise-book towards me she said,

'You must sign, dear.'

'Sign? Sign what?' I asked in bewilderment.

'Write down "I spoke in geography" and sign your name, dear,' she replied, hurriedly resuming a question on the Welland canal.

Soon there was a mid-morning interval, and I asked a girl what on earth this kind of thing meant. She explained that we had to write down what we had done wrong and sign our name every time we broke a rule.

'Yes, and then what happens?' I asked.

'Oh nothing more than that. We just sign.'

'Is that all? How my brothers will laugh!'

'Your brothers may, but *you* won't when your parents see at the end of the term "Reported for breach of Regulations – 23 times". So look out.'

In what deep dejection I got home that day and tried to hide my bitter disappointment from Mother! But mothers always scent low spirits, and she refrained from asking too much. I was glad that Tony was in Cornwall and need not know that she was paying such high fees for so little. I showed Mother the list of Rules that had been presented to each new girl (as well as posted at intervals about the building). It was in small print and double columns, like the blue by-laws in the trams. Mother laughed and thought them 'rather excessive'.

Those were the permanent rules, but almost every day a new one appeared in a corridor, in large sprawling home-made lettering — such as: 'Broken needles must not be thrown on the floor.' They were so many that they ceased to attract attention and got caught up into the decorative scheme. 'I can't possibly remember all these,' thought I, 'so I shan't bother about them.' A few of them, however, still remain in my memory: Every book had to be covered (a different colour for each subject). No girl might bring a pen to school (was this to avoid ink-stains?). We were forbidden to get wet on the way to school, to walk more than three in a row, to drop a pencil-box, leave a book at home, hang aboot-bag by only one loop, run down the stairs, speak in class. As for speaking, it would have been easier to enumerate the few places where we were permitted to speak than those where talking was forbidden. The ideas were sensible, but why make rules about them? One felt that if a girl were to knock over the blackboard by mistake there would be a rule against it the next day.

Arriving early one morning I was alone in a corridor and chanced to drop my pencil-box. 'Thank goodness,' thought I, 'there's no one to hear it.' Hardly had this crossed my mind when the voice of Miss Begbie came from some distant cloak-room, 'You must sign for that, dear.'

The book in which all these crimes were recorded had an ominous title — 'The Appearing Book', smacking not a little of the Day of Judgement. As the culprit was left to state her own crime, some amusing things were entered in the book that may well puzzle future students of nineteenth-century educa-tion. 'I marched with the wrong foot' was the way a girl expressed her failure to keep step. 'I was four in a row', 'I spoke in French', 'I called out in Latin'. A technical distinction appears here; to *speak* was to talk to another girl, while to *call out* was to answer before you were asked. 'I left my heart at home' referred to a diagram for physiology.

On the rare occasions of a Form's going half a term without a signature, it was awarded a Gratification. This was a half-hour to be spent in any way the girls chose. Only once did this boon come my way, and there was much hesitation among the class, and searching for some noble idea in the way of recreation. In a pause I exclaimed loudly, 'Well, *I* should like a romp.' Amid much laughter the others then confessed to a similar wish, and blessed me heartily as we all trooped off to the gymnasium and let ourselves go.

Now and again a girl who had collected too many signatures would have an imposition, a piece of French to write or learn, but this was so rare that I only once observed a girl doing it. And anyhow it was nothing to what might befall any one at any moment: this was what the boys called a 'jaw'. But I don't believe any boy since the world began has ever known what a jaw can be. It needed Miss Buss to give a full content to the term. I never experienced it myself, but heard tales enough of poor girls reduced to sobs and almost hysterics as they bent under the storm that went on and on and on.

⁂

Coming into the school at the age of sixteen I saw its glaring faults and absurdities. The whole seemed to me an elaborate machine for doing the minimum of useful things with the maximum of fuss. I didn't see then, as I saw later, that Miss Buss was faced by a herculean task. The endless anxieties she caused her pupils were as nothing to her own big anxiety. She was a pioneer, and almost single-handed, in getting some kind of systematic education for girls. She had no school to copy, no precedent of any kind. Her private school had been so successful that she found herself before long with five hundred girls – all to be taught something and to be trained along Victorian lines of good behaviour.

To be taught something – but what? Negatively the problem was easy. All the hitherto satisfactory ideals of accomplishments and 'finishing' must be wiped out, but what was to take their place? While the education of boys had been gradually shaped from ancient times, engaging the attention of philosophers, that of girls had as a rule no other aim beyond making them pleasing to men. This idea was to Miss Buss anathema, and she failed to see all its great possibilities when really well done. To be deeply pleasing to a husband, and widely pleasing to other men, seems to me as good an ideal as a woman can have. But instead of facing squarely the real needs of future wives and mothers, as the vast majority of girls were to be, Miss Buss seized the tempting instrument at her hand – the stimulus to mental ambition afforded by outside examinations. By this means the curriculum was ready-made. And thus, for better or worse, the education of girls became a feeble imitation of what the boys were doing, for the public examinations made no distinction of sex, and no woman's voice was heard at the examination boards.

# 15

# UNDER GRACE

IF the weather during my first term might be described as 'cloudy with bright intervals', one day shortly after the beginning of my second term the sky changed to 'set fair'.

A school official burst into our room and asked in an offhand way, as though expecting no response, 'Has any girl here ever done any Latin?' I put up my hand, the only one, as well as I remember. On further questioning, I admitted having read a good deal of Caesar, two or three books of the *Aeneid*, and some Livy. These points were taken down and the official departed. We were so used to such sudden questionnaires, demanding statistics as to our birth-place, full Christian names, father's initials (if dead, put 'none'), and so on, that I thought no more of it, not even mentioning the incident to Mother, the ever eager listener to the smallest items of news.

Next day at the mid-morning interval we were lined up as usual in rows, and indulging in as much talking as we could squeeze into the time while we ate our halfpenny buns, when Miss Buss entered. There was a slight sensation in the ranks, for her presence in the dining-room was unusual, and a stormy petrel. An underling in her wake called out 'Mary Thomas'.

'Now you're for it,' said the girl standing by me. 'What have you been up to?'

'I can't think,' said I, as I started off.

'Mind you stand up to her,' was the parting injunction.

Miss Buss was evidently in one of her unpleasant moods. But I was fairly comfortable in my conscience and looked her full in the eye.

'What was your last school?' she barked at me.

'Oh, only a private school,' said I in a deprecatory tone as an attempt at delicate flattery.

'What is its *name*, I said. Answer my question.'

I gave her the name, but it obviously conveyed no idea to her, and I wondered why she wanted to know it. Then she shot at me almost venomously:

'How long have you been learning Latin?'

'I can't remember. Mother began me when I was about six, and I have been doing it off and on ever since, chiefly with my brother.' Then something in her expression gave me the clue to her ill-temper and induced me to add 'Not much at the school'.

At this a look of relief crossed her face and she visibly relaxed, but pulled herself up again, glared at me for a moment or two in silence and then snapped out:

'Go back to your place.'

'What was the matter?' was the inquiry of my neighbours in the line.

'Nothing much. She only wanted to know the name of my last school, and exactly how long I had been learning Latin, just to fill in some of those eternal forms, I expect.'

On our return to the classroom I was ordered to take the books out of my desk and go to the Upper Fifth. This must mean a sudden 'remove', and staggering mentally under the idea and physically under the books I made my way to the room that was actually next-door to the Sixth! Here I was cordially welcomed by the form mistress and helped quite graciously to a vacant desk. A lesson was in progress on the derivation of French words. I found this amusing, for it was quite a new idea to me that other countries had 'derivations' for their words. I gained much kudos from being able to contribute several Latin words in the accusative, which appeared to be in great demand. Towards the end of the morning one of my new comrades was told off to show me what the home-work would be for the next day. I went home on the wings of an eagle, giving Mother the full dramatic scene as I ate my dinner.

She and I turned with anxiety to examine the new home-work, and found it difficult in some ways, but not beyond our joint efforts. Mother came out strong over a tricky bit of French composition, and the exhilaration of my 'remove' made everything seem fun to us. The mere look of the Cicero text (lent me for the day) was like the rattling of spears to the war-horse. 'Bless you, Mother,' said I, 'for having started me in Latin so early, for that's what got me my move.'

The next day I felt more at ease and able to look round the room. The sight that attracted me more than any other was a girl with a mass of red-gold hair and, whenever I caught her eye, a jolly smile. We gravitated to one another in the lunch interval, and exchanged our names and gossip. This Mary Wood had known no other school, had been under Miss Buss since childhood, and thought everything perfect. She had reached the Upper Fifth as she said, 'in a proper and orderly way, not like you "by the earthquake".' I was glad she knew her *Alice*, and we soon found many books and tastes in common. When I

*The Sisters, by William Jabez Muckley*

demurred to so many rules all over the place, she told me that it was nothing to what they endured in the lower part of the school. Here a wooden instrument called a 'clacker' was in use for giving commands – to stand, put pencils down, 'hands away', pass out, and so on. It was used even for punctuation in a dictation exercise: one clack, a comma; two clacks, a semicolon; three, a colon; four, a full-stop. I had heard this clacker clacking in the distance and had wondered what it was. But I gathered that as one went up the school the discipline was relaxed bit by bit, and to my relief I found that learning daily portions of poetry was not required in the Upper Fifth.

There was an announcement one morning that Mary Wood was to have a day's absence for a sister's wedding, and would some one volunteer to send her the particulars of home-work by post? I immediately offered, and stepped up to my new-found friend to get her address. Only recently, while writing this book, I recalled this incident to her, and she said, 'Yes, indeed I remember it well, and the angry tears I shed at being obliged to stay away from school for even that one day.' Surely the oddest of reasons for tears at a wedding.

When the half-term holiday came Mother asked me whether I would like to invite a schoolfellow to tea.

'Very much,' said I. 'There are lots of jolly girls, only I have no idea where any of them live.' Then suddenly remembering that I had Mary Wood's address in my note-book, I looked it up and decided that it couldn't be very far, for it was in Camden Road itself. So off I started to fetch her. But Camden Road seemed to stretch endlessly, and the numbers on one side bore no relation to those on the other. I persevered until I reached No.267, and found it to be an imposing house with a large garden. Rather shyly I knocked at the door, little thinking how often I should come to it, how dear all its inmates were to become to me, and how I should be married from it.

Mary was more than willing to come back to tea with me, and insisted on bringing her shoes to change, in spite of my assurances that our family didn't mind mud. Mother was much struck with this bit of thoughtfulness, and took a great liking to Mary at once. There was special tea for us, and Mary was delighted with the boys' study, and Charles's pictures and our family magazine. Thus began a friendship of over fifty years between our families, that has had no break nor even suspension.

※

Although we were all very friendly together in the Sixth, Mary Wood's was the only house that I visited. She and I used to spend any half-term or odd holiday together, she with me and my brothers or I with her and her sisters. I had no sister, she no brother, so it fitted well, and all through life she has been more of a sister to me than any one else. We were never very emotional in our friendship, and that is perhaps why it wore so well. Her people came from Shetland, and that always seemed romantic to me. Her mother used to tell me of the ways of the country people there, and these had the same tang of reality that we had in Cornwall. The inhabitants of Lerwick, she said, are not at all Scottish, but speak a mixture of English and Norsk. When my aunt Tony was staying with us she hailed Mary ecstatically:

'Why, my dear child, you are thoroughly Norsk – the shape of your head, your peculiar type of golden hair, yes, and your ready laugh.' It was a disappointment to Tony that Mary could not speak Norsk, for they could have conversed together – the rarest of treats for Tony.

Of Mary's sisters I was rather in awe. The eldest was an artist who exhibited regularly in the Academy; but she was very jolly to us younger ones and amused us with acting and reciting. Another sister had been to Girton and was reading for a medical degree, and to this day I have not quite overcome my original fear of her. Mary also had a twin sister, whose chief ambition was to leave school and pursue her art studies. She never expressed the least interest in any school subject, having remained in the same slough of despond into which I fell on my first arrival, although (by some scholastic hydraulic pressure) she reached one of the Fifth Forms. But for the grace of God, I thought, or rather for my mother's starting me in Latin, there goes Mary Thomas.

The person I ought to have been frightened of was their father. But I have never felt alarmed at a man, and although Mr Wood was in aspect and manner quite forbidding, I took great delight in him, and I think he was surprised and amused to find any one to treat him so cavalierly. Full of fierceness and severity of criticism, especially against radicals and nonconformists, he would break his brooding silence at any moment with some caustic remark. At breakfast, buried behind *The Times*, he would read out a bit of the less cheerful news here and there. If Gladstone's name occurred he would mutter in brackets, 'Damned old scoundrel'. One morning, in a specially morose mood, he read out to the family the statistics of the inmates of the workhouses: so many agricultural labourers, so many bank-clerks, so many plasterers . . . Seeing the gloom round the table deepening, I broke in:

'Does it say how many barristers?'

At this he ran his eye over the list again, looked solemnly at me over his spectacles and replied, 'I see no mention of them. The truth is that there are so many that they gave up counting them'; and then he added that his net income during the past year had been fourpence-halfpenny.

When I was spending a weekend there he would take Mary and me to the Temple on Sunday morning, and before Service would take us into his chambers at No.1 Hare Court. These were on the ground-floor and looking into the old court. Everything here had a peculiar attraction for me — the portraits of famous judges on the walls, the rows of Law books on the shelves, the musty aroma of the room, and, above all, the scope for imagination of all the fateful conferences and decisions that went on in 'chambers'. I made up my mind that if ever I married it must be to a barrister, little thinking that by sheer coincidence that very room was to be my husband's.

Mr Wood's dislike of nonconformity was very much the same as my father's — an objection to anything openly perfervid in the religious line, but unlike my father he fell in with the Victorian custom of assembling the family and servants for prayers every evening. They were conducted in the same off-hand style in which he used to look into his hat for a few moments before the Service in the Temple. We read round a verse each of the Bible, during which my interest was absorbed in watching for Libby's trouble with difficult words. Then followed a few short prayers, mumbled so hastily that I had the impression of his being ashamed to bother the Almighty and that he was hoping not to secure attention. A little girl on a visit there had been warned to be very quiet during the proceedings, and in the middle we heard a shocked whisper, 'Mamma naughty bo nose'.

Libby had been their cook for untold years, and seemed to rule the entire establishment. Her name was the children's corruption of Elizabeth, and with them she remained to her dying day. Mary and Ursula (her twin sister) and I were not considered old enough to be present at the family evening dinner, and had supper by ourselves in the study; but Libby would always sail in with some tit-bits for us, such as gooseberry-fool or lemon-sponge. We could also make a raid on the kitchen at any time, and be sure of good sustenance from an over-indulgent Libby. The housemaid had also been with them from babyhood, for there were stories of her sternness in giving the twins their bath, allowing no splashing till the end, when she would exclaim, 'Now waller'. Her standard of morality was high and she never laughed, while Libby, a devotee of Spurgeon, would break into joyful smiles on any provocation, and I gave her plenty.

*Hampstead, by Atkinson Grimshaw*

Except Mary Wood, who was definitely fixed for Girton, we were all rather wondering about our future. Miss Buss took a personal interest in all her 'leavers', and had shrewd ideas about suitable careers. At this time a new opening for women attracted her attention – the instruction of the deaf and dumb. Clever and sensitive fingers were specially desirable for this work, and one of the girls at school in my time was well endowed in this way and seemed indicated as a pioneer. When approached on the subject, however, she repudiated the idea entirely. But Miss Buss was not so easily put off and pressed upon her again and again the glories of such a noble career. At last, annoyed beyond endurance, the girl burst out:

'No, I will not teach the deaf and dumb. I would rather be a . . .' There was a pause and the expected word was 'hangman', but the word that came out was 'dentist'. This was a curious case of the subconscious mind getting a chance when one is in a temper; for she told us that on the way home, feeling calmer, she said to herself, 'A dentist? Whatever made me say that? Why, that is the very thing I should like to be!' She then went to Miss Buss to unfold her ambition.

'How absurd, child! There is no such thing as a woman dentist.'

Determined, however, to be a dentist if it were at all possible, the girl got her parents to make inquiries. They drew blank in England, but found that there was a chance of admission in Edinburgh. They managed to send her to Edinburgh, where she came out head of the list in the final examination. Miss Buss of course congratulated her, and also showed generosity by acknowledging her own stupidity in having tried to drive her into a career she disliked. Truly Miss Buss illustrates the saying that 'personality is a tissue of surprises'.

The majority of us who had matriculated faced the fact that we should have to become teachers. It seemed a fairly pleasing prospect, mainly consisting, as far as work went, in talking and putting red crosses on other people's mistakes. But we now heard that you could be *taught* how to teach – a funny idea. Soon a chance arose for me to hear more about it. Along with some other enthusiasts Miss Buss was trying to raise teaching into a real profession, like Law or Medicine. To this end they formed a Society, called eventually 'The Teachers' Guild'. Of course, the most irritating stumbling-block to such a scheme was the amused indifference of man-kind. My brother Tom seemed to Miss Buss a promising convert, and in the hope of getting him interested she invited me to bring him to one of the first meetings of the infant Society.

So he and I made our way to the appointed spot – one of London's gloomiest halls (in Farringdon Street, as well as I remember). About a hundred earnest-looking people, mostly women, were percolating into the seats, and in due time the platform was occupied by a few men of weight. A bishop spoke at great length, and was followed by two public school masters – not over-enthusiastic. The weather was dull, the audience heavy-going, and the speeches in sympathy with both. But Tom could suck fun from the most unpromising material, and the more melancholy the speakers became the more absurd they seemed, and the more sidelong glances Tom shot at me. At last Mrs Bryant rose to speak, and put some life into the audience with a breezy talk. She evidently was speaking from deep conviction and a full heart; but she became so involved in a tirade against the indifference of the world at large to 'this great question', with many an 'if only' and 'if however', that Tom whispered to me in apparent alarm, 'She's forgotten her apodosis'. I believe the lady on my other side thought it was some part of her toilet.

Probably Miss Buss and Mrs Bryant were disappointed with that meeting. They were doers rather than talkers, and a new scheme was fertilizing in their busy brains. 'Here we are,' they were saying, 'with a big school, and a deplorable deficiency of really good teachers. Let us pick a few of our best girls and venture some money in training them properly for their work.' The Training Colleges already in being did not satisfy their ideals, and they looked round for some appropriate place and for some appropriate person. Undoubtedly Cambridge, with its colleges for women as encouragement, was the right background for general culture. And a certain Miss E.P. Hughes, one of the most brilliant of Newnham's graduates, was the exactly right one to be the Principal. To her could be entrusted the entire working out of the scheme.

Of course I knew nothing at the time of all this activity behind the scenes. The first news of it that reached me was that I had been selected as one of the four North Londoners who were to be among the first students in 'a new college at Cambridge'.

*A Swift Patent Reservoir Pen*

# 16

# MY FIRST POST, 1886

*Molly went to Cambridge in 1885, in the first batch of fourteen women students at the Training College for teachers. The next year, after an interview in a borrowed bonnet, she was assigned to a school in Darlington.*

'POLAM Darlington.' These two words were all the information I had about my new work; for when I was in that bonnet I took in very little as to my duties. Mother was all alive at the idea of coming with me and seeing new kinds of people. 'Very outspoken' was the characteristic she had both heard and experienced of the north country. We could not actually live together, since it was a resident post, but the headmistress recommended to us a trustworthy landlady not far from the school. So with this name and address we started off together from King's Cross in good spirits. On our arrival in Darlington we drove first to Mother's lodgings.

The word 'lodgings' casts a gloom over most people, but to me it brings a memory of a large sunny room in West Terrace, and of an old lady and her daughter of gentlest nature, who laid themselves out to have Mother well-fed and tended. Indeed, I gathered that a real affection grew up between them, for Mrs Steele used to have heart to heart talks with Mother about times and customs that were past; she was too old for much active work, and I think Miss Steele was grateful for mother's friendliness with her. Her stay with these people was one of the really happy periods of Mother's life, for she was free from cares, had time for reading and sketching, and had my daily visit with school gossip to look forward to.

By another stroke of luck it chanced that my brother Tom, who had not long been married, came north at the same time that we did. As classics master in Middlesbrough High School he was within a short railway journey of Darlington, and very seldom a week passed when he didn't manage to run over to see us.

*Packing a Trunk, by Frank Hobden*

Polam was not a private school, but was under the management of some kind of Church Trust, about which I was never clear. 'Polam' was the name of a large house in extensive and well laid-out grounds, including lawns, woods, and a good-sized lake. Schoolrooms had been added as a kind of wing, beyond the conservatories; the pupils numbered about seventy day-girls and over a dozen boarders; the staff consisted of the headmistress, who did Arithmetic and what she called 'a little mathematics', a Fräulein for French and German, visiting masters for Music and Drawing, and me for the rest.

What appalled me was not the number of subjects assigned to me, but the elder boarders. I met these girls at supper on my arrival, and barely slept for fear of facing them in class on the morrow. Big girls they were, in long skirts and with their hair done up, looking older than I did, or felt, and apparently far more women of the world.

My first lesson was with a younger class, and it passed off without much trouble, but for the second hour I was faced by two rows of those formidable young women for a geography lesson. Few animals are more awe-inspiring than a group of English schoolgirls who are taking your measure. I had had no opportunity for preparing a lesson, so it was with assumed nonchalance that I asked: 'What country are you to be taking next?'

'Italy,' was the lack-lustre reply.

'Oh, then we shall want a map,' said I as casually as I could, but thanking my stars for that map of the Mediterranean I had practised for the matriculation. With careless ease I turned to the board and executed the western half of my masterpiece. When I looked round the class had come to life, and amazement sat on the previously disdainful faces.

'Did you do that out of your head?' exclaimed one girl.

At this I spread out my hands, to show that there was no book or atlas near me, and said, 'No deception, ladies and gentlemen.' When a laugh greeted this my nervousness had entirely gone, and we all set out to fill up the map, as by a kind of dentistry I extracted a few of the 'natural features' from the class. While the Alps were being laboriously chalked in, I muttered 'Poor Hannibal!'

Overhearing this the girl nearest me said, 'Hannibal? That's a funny name — it's what our old horse at home is called.'

'Funny name!' I said, 'but surely you know who Hannibal was?'

Not one of the class had so much as heard of him, and when I looked shocked and said, 'Why, he was one of the greatest men that ever lived' there was an urgent demand, 'Do tell us about him.' Only too glad to get away from the products and industries of Italy (which I felt to be approaching) I plunged into Hannibal's boyhood, and took those girls with genuine excitement from Africa through Spain, over the Rhône (with a sketch of an elephant thrown in), across the Alps and down to victory in Italy. Then pacing up and down the classroom I acted Fabius, wintered in Capua, made a crescendo to Cannae, cursed the authorities in Carthage, and was hesitating about attacking Rome when the bell rang to the accompaniment of groans.

I had taken my first fence, but there was another to be taken that I had not even suspected. During those first few days one after another of the elder boarders would come up to me at any odd time of the day to ask me the meaning of something — anthropomorphic, bicentenary, protoplasm, and other long words. I gave the meaning briefly, but one day it was 'upanishad'.

'I have no idea what that means,' said I, 'fetch the book where you came across it, and we shall be able to give a guess at it from the context.'

The expectant group looked uncomfortable, and then confessed that they hadn't got any book, but had picked it out of the dictionary. Then they told me that my predecessor had always explained a word if she knew it, but if she didn't she would not admit her ignorance but would say, 'Don't bother me about a mere word, look it up in the dictionary, dear.' This sport lost its zest as soon as I admitted ignorance, and we laughed together at the absurdity of pretending to know everything.

After this we were friends, and sincerer friends than those few elder girls I have never had. They began to take an interest in their work, and induced me to join in their play, which chiefly consisted of tennis and rowing on the lake. They had the north-country outspokenness and were extremely matter-of-fact; their intelligence and interest in almost any topic gave a real fillip to my daily round. One day the eldest came to me, with the others attendant, to say, 'Miss Thomas, dear, we think something ought to be done about your hair.' Ever since leaving Cambridge I had been trying to look more grown-up by cajoling my hair into a knob with hairpins, but with the utmost pulling I could produce nothing bigger than half a crown. So I asked these girls to try their hand at it. After several efforts they came to the conclusion that it would be better cropped short. When I saw Tom at the weekend I consulted him on the point. 'Well dear,' said he, 'you may as well have it cut, for you couldn't possibly look worse than you do now.' And on this hint I cut.

⁂

The headmistress was a martinet about her assistants, but lazy about her own work, and as the term went on I found that she was pushing ever more and more duties on me. For instance, the visiting master for Drawing was obliged to take a large class that spread over two communicating rooms. When he was in one room the discipline in the other declined. So I was asked to give up my free afternoon – usually spent in a walk with Mother – in order to sit in the younger Drawing division and eye the children. I soon found that what they wanted was not eyeing but something interesting to draw. After a little furtive helping I began to supply this need, and the master was only too glad to leave me to it, and as soon as the headmistress heard of it she asked me to take on the teaching of Drawing regularly. I ought to have borne in mind Tony's dictum about servants: 'I never think much of a servant who is willing to undertake duties that she has not bargained for.'

Mother had noticed that I was getting fagged out with the ups and downs of my first term, and she had been busy devising a summer holiday. A little family reunion seemed to be indicated, for Tom was within easy reach, and Charles could very likely come from Bedford. In her varied explorations she had come across a little fishing village called Runswick Bay, that fascinated her artistic sense. She thought it would also please Charles, who had written to say that if

*A Game of Tennis, by Spencer Gore*

we could get some nice, damp, inconvenient habitation that was picturesque, he would join us. It certainly filled the bill as far as being damp, inconvenient, and picturesque, but it failed on the point of habitation. Mother could find no cottage that she could fancy herself entering, let alone asking for 'rooms' in it. She climbed back to Hinderwell again, determined to try some other place along that lovely coast. There was a long wait for the next train, and she passed the time by confiding her disappointment to the stationmaster.

'Well, mum,' said he, 'why not put up here in the station?'

'Good gracious!' said Mother, 'I had no idea that any one could *live* in a station.'

He thereupon showed her what he could do. There was a real sitting-room, right on the platform, most convincing, with lace curtains, and fern, and red table-cloth, and a fine view of the railway and signal-box. Tucked away behind the little Booking-office was a smaller room that would do for meals, and a tiny kitchen beyond. Along the platform was a waiting-room that could be used as an extra sitting-room if required. Over all, going the length of the platform, were three bedrooms. It was like a house in a two-dimensional land. He ended the tour of inspection by saying, 'My wife is a good cook, and you will be very comfortable.'

And so we were. Tom and his wife, and Charles and I, and most certainly Mother, were all of us children enough to be enchanted with our new mode of life, and the fun never grew stale. Four trains passed to and fro every day – two 'to' and two 'fro'. One was due to rattle in during our dinner hour, and we always had to run to the front room to see how many alighted. There was usually a half-finished picture on Charles's easel by the window, and we enjoyed watching the passengers trying to look at it without seeming inquisitive. Most of them had come for an afternoon at the sea.

Runswick Bay was enough to attract any one, when once the approach to it had been overcome. A rough stony lane led down to it from Hinderwell, and after that a path went steeply down to the sea, winding in and out among the primitive fishermen's cottages. To say that it smelt like Caliban would be merely flattery. But what matter? Once down by the sea and the place was a paradise. The insanitary old cottages took on another aspect, nestling among the rocks and verdure of the hillside; and in the foreground there were the boats and fishing-tackle on the firm white sand in a brilliant setting of sea and sky. Mother and Charles were busy sketching all day long, whilst we others read and bathed and basked. I had brought *Rudder Grange* with me, and recommended it to Charles, because it described the same kind of odd dwelling that we were in. Mother and I slept in the room next to his, and one morning we were alarmed by great bursts of laughter coming from him. We were alarmed because it was so extraordinary. Charles made others laugh but never laughed himself, and we feared that something serious was the matter – a brain attack or something. I jumped up and knocked at his door.

'What's the matter, Charles?'

'Oh,' he managed to say with fresh outbursts, 'we are like the people in *Rudder Grange*, we live in a stationary wash-tub!'

Mother and I liked to hear that laughter, for it was a sign of the new enjoyment of life that had begun for Charles. We had been troubled about him long enough. On my father's death he was a sensitive, highly-strung boy of seventeen, the only one of us likely to shine, and he was obliged to take the only job that offered – one that involved long hours as a clerk in a sordid factory in Kingsland. He got away from it after a few months, but not until it had half killed him, body and spirit. But now he liked his work and friends at Bedford,

*Runswick Bay, 1886, from a watercolour by Charles*

and had ample chance to carry on his painting.

Owing to the different dates of term beginning, Charles had to leave for Bedford two days before we had to return to Darlington. I went to the little station at Sandsend to see him off.

'Is there any chance of your coming south?' he asked, 'because I want you to meet Hughes, and he wants to meet you.'

'I shall have to go to Cambridge for my Teacher's Diploma, but not till next year, because you can't take it till you're twenty, and I shan't be that till October.'

'All right. Then we must put off the meeting till then. We will manage for you to have a weekend at Bedford just before or after, as it suits. Our headmaster and his wife know about you and will gladly put you up.'

The train came in, and to my intense surprise he gave me an affectionate kiss, the only one, so far as I remember, that he ever gave me. That little scene is impressed on my memory, for I never saw him again.

One evening in June I had skipped away from the school and its worries to have an hour with Mother. She was showing me a half-finished water-colour. 'Now remember what Charles says, don't go touching it up indoors, but go to the same spot tomorrow and get the same lights.' I was just saying this when Miss Steele came in with a telegram. It was from Bedford – 'your son very ill – come at once'.

'Pack your handbag, Mother, while I run to the station to see when the next train goes.'

It was not till midnight, so there was time for me to go round to the school to let them know I should be late, and unfortunately time for Mother and me to speculate on what the illness could be. It was a bolt from the blue, for although Charles had been delicate from his birth he had never been definitely ill. And we had had the rosiest accounts from him lately. He had spent the Easter holiday in a sketching tour in Devon and Cornwall, and since then he had begun a series of water-colours to illustrate a book he meant to write on the countryside of Bunyan.

Next day I had a telegram from Mother at Bedford that was obviously vague, so I guessed things were serious, and wrote at once to Tony in Cornwall and to Dym in Plymouth, asking them to go to Bedford at once. The elder girls at school were splendidly sympathetic, saying very little and working very hard during lesson time. It was two mornings later that I was giving them Latin, in a front room, and we all saw a telegraph boy walking up to the front door. In a minute a servant came into the room and handed me a telegram. They were rare things in those days, and there was little doubt what the message was. Without opening it I thrust it into my pocket, and shall never forget the look those few girls gave me before they all bent over their conditional sentences as if nothing else in the world mattered. North-country people may be brusque and outspoken, but for a sure touch of sympathy I have seldom seen the behaviour of that class equalled.

Charles had died that morning. Mother and Tony came on together to Darlington after a few days, and I had more particulars from them. He had been taken suddenly ill, and though apparently conscious now and again, he was never able to speak. Mother, Dym, Tony, the school nurse, and one of the masters took turns to watch by his bedside. This master had been with him through the night before he died, and to him (I learnt long afterwards) Charles had made with painful effort a gesture of affection.

Mother, Dym, and Tony were full of gratitude to this master, 'a Mr Hughes', who acted like a son in helping them to arrange Charles's few belongings and pack his many pictures. They were anxious to have him buried in the beautiful little churchyard of Elstow, but there were serious local difficulties, and it was not until they had shown his pictures of the village and its surroundings that they obtained permission.

We ought to have been equally grateful to Tony, but she was always on the spot in any trouble, and we had come to look upon her as part of the scheme of Providence. To her Charles's death was as great a blow as to Mother – greater, I think, for she had understood his artistic capability from his early boyhood, and had continually urged him to devote all his energy to it. And now to lose him at the age of twenty-four, just when he had been able to sell many of his pictures, and was hoping to give up school work, have a little studio some-where in Cornwall, and paint to his heart's delight! It is surely a nice point whether a physical mother or a spiritual mother feels bereavement more.

'That Mr Hughes you speak of,' said I, 'is the one Charles talked to me about, and wanted me to meet this summer.'

'Yes,' said Tony, 'he seemed to know a good deal about you. And so did the headmaster and his wife. They have made all arrangements for you to come to spend a weekend when you have to go to Cambridge for your examination.'

'Oh well, that's all off now – without Charles there's no point in going to Bedford.'

'Yes, but they think you would like to see his grave in that lovely church-yard, the chapel where he played the organ for the boys, and his room and everything, and meet his friends. They sent a most pressing invitation, didn't they, Mary?'

'They couldn't have been kinder,' said mother, 'but Molly must decide for herself whether to go or not.'

When Tony and I were alone, 'You go, dear,' said she, 'Mr Hughes is so anxious to see you, and he has been so good to us that I think you really *ought*.'

So it was arranged that I should spend the weekend (before the examina-tion) at Bedford, towards the end of June. That examination was rather a godsend at the moment, for it took my mind off other things. I had to look up a few facts about Vittorino da Feltre, and Gerson, and Jacotot, and people like that. I could do plenty of jargon about Sensation and Perception and the Laws of Association, but did not consider the bits of psychology I had picked up while teaching to be 'examination-worthy' or that they would go down with a Cambridge examiner. Methods of teaching had become a part of me, but I had to look up the 'rules for questioning' so as to have them at my finger-tips.

As the time drew near, any nervousness about the examination was lost in my nervousness at encountering all the strangers at Bedford, and the large staff of masters.

'But the headmaster's wife is delightful, and has three dear little children, and Mr Hughes writes to say that he will meet you at the station.'

'How shall I know him? What is he like?'

'Short and thick-set,' said Mother, 'very plain, dark, a good bit older than Charles, short-sighted, and very severe-looking, not jolly a bit. He told us that Charles used to call him Diogenes, because he took such a gloomy view of life.'

'I don't care what he's like – he was good to Charles,' put in Tony.

'He has a big moustache,' went on Mother ruthlessly, 'and he plays the fiddle. He tries to do water-colours, but of course is no good at it.'

I was prepared for something pretty bad, deceived as ever by Mother's trick of putting one off what she really hoped one would like. To stave off nervousness on the journey I went over all the bits of 'book-psychology' that I could think of. As the train slowed down for Bedford, I took my small bag from the rack and braced myself for the task of hunting about the crowd for a man who presumably would be looking vaguely expectant. What if I made a mistake, or saw no one at all likely? We drew up, and I jumped down into the usual platform medley. I had hardly landed when someone came briskly up to me, shook me firmly by the hand, and said, 'There's a cab waiting. What luggage have you?' I handed him my bag with, 'That's all. Are you Mr Hughes?' 'Yes, come along.' The headmaster's wife was in the cab, and greeted me with, 'You will be just in time for tea, and they're all expecting you. There's a big cricket match on.'

That tea on the lawn was ambrosial; it was a glorious June afternoon, and the men in their white flannels reminded me of my childhood when my father used to have cricketing parties; and at this time there was a specially grand tea on account of the Jubilee celebrations. No one mentioned Charles, but I felt from the manner of each of the masters as he chatted to me that he was doing his best to make my visit a jolly one – all except Mr Hughes, who had disappeared. As they were dispersing again for cricket I heard his voice at my side, 'I want you to see the shadow cast by the big tree on Elstow church. Your brother made several studies of it. In this light it will be showing to perfection. Come along, and these roses I have just been gathering are for you to put on his grave.'

Our walk of about a quarter of a mile lay through some cornfields, in full view of the church and the shadow on it. We passed the village green and the old moot-house and threaded our way through the churchyard to the newly made grave. As I laid the roses on it Mr Hughes said, 'He will wake and remember and understand.' Those were practically the only words spoken during that walk. The evening and the next day were made as bright as possible for me by my host and hostess, till Sunday afternoon when I had to leave for Cambridge. Mr Hughes saw me off at the station, still silent, but just before the train came in he said, 'Your brother was teaching me to paint, but I'm no hand at it. I've made a little sketch of the corner of the churchyard showing his grave, where we stood together on Saturday, and perhaps you will accept it; but it is only for you, and not to be shown to any one else.' He then handed it to me and silence fell again. But just as the train was about to start he said: 'We haven't talked much, you and I, have we? But never mind, we have all the future before us.'

*Arthur Hughes, from a sepia sketch by Molly*

# 17

# AT HELL'S MOUTH, 1887

ON my return I found that affairs in Darlington had been getting worse, and there was a common rumour in the town that the Association to which the school belonged was bankrupt. The tradespeople were refusing to supply what little food was ordered. The pupils stayed on with the dumb acquiescence that young people usually show. We teachers stayed on for fear of risking our salaries. But one day we were informed by the headmistress that the school could not be carried on even to the end of the current term, and that there would not be a penny of salary for any one. This left the poor Fräulein all but penniless, and if it hadn't been for Tony's help she would not have had enough to get home to Germany. Tony as usual took matters into her own hand, and insisted on carrying off Mother and me at once to Cornwall. I was sorry to say good-bye to my faithful friends, those elder girls, and Mother felt parting from the Steeles. Otherwise we were delighted to shake the dust of Darlington from our heels as we steamed out of Bank-top Station. Our spirits rose higher the nearer we approached the west country and heard the soft tones of the people – such a contrast to the harsher voices of the north. How we hailed the little white-washed cottages at Saltash, and when I saw Carn Brea rising out of the evening mist I felt like a crusader sighting Jerusalem.

Lack of money had prevented our going to Cornwall for several years, and I felt that my cousins and I would be almost strangers to one another. I asked Tony whether they had changed much.

'It is you who have done the changing, dear. I think they are rather dreading you as a "modern girl".'

'What a funny idea! What *is* a modern girl, Tony?'

'Well you have been to a big modern school, and to Cambridge, and they think you know a lot, and may ride the high horse – absurd idea, of course.'

Tony had a little surprise for me one day. When she was in Bedford she had taken a great liking to Arthur Hughes (not only out of gratitude for his kindness to Charles), and she had begged him to come down to Reskadinnick for a visit. And now she had a letter from him saying he could run down from his home in Wales for a few days – ten at most – and if convenient he would come at once. 'We must do our best to make him welcome, and show him something of the Cornwall that Charles loved so dearly. I've written to tell him to come as soon as he likes.'

As it turned out there was little left for Mother and me to do in the way of making him welcome. The cousins at Reskadinnick did all. They took him on expeditions to the points of interest, and it was only in brief snatches that I had any chat with him. . . .

Mother and I were both invited to a 'musical evening' at Reskadinnick, and Mr Hughes, who never went anywhere without his fiddle, was able to add considerably to the entertainment. A trio of Gounod's *Ave Maria*, with one cousin at the piano, another singing, and the fiddle accompanying, pleased me greatly, and at the end I asked Mr Hughes to pass me the musical score to look at. He came over to me and handed it with the words, very much in inverted commas, "and afterward, what else?" He knew that I should recognize the quotation from *The Patriot*, and that no one else would.

Towards the end of his visit, for some unknown and blessed reason (probably due to Tony, like most good things in my life), I was asked to go for an evening drive to the Cliffs with the Reskadinnick cousins. We started after an early tea, the time of day just right for colour; the weather was at its best, heather in full bloom, sea ultramarine laced with emerald, rocks looking defiant as the great breakers tossed their foam over them. As was customary, the wagonette pulled up at Hell's Mouth, our show-piece, so that we might all get out to look down.

Knowing every inch of the ground from my childhood, I ran on ahead of the others, all eager to show our visitor the way to do it. The ritual was to run up to the edge of the cliff and then lie full length, with head over, so as to gaze in safety at the cauldron of raging sea below. Before lying down I turned to hail the others coming up. To my surprise Arthur Hughes was in front of them all, running and looking horribly scared.

'What is the matter?' I asked.

'Oh!' he gasped, 'I thought you were bound to go over – running at the edge like that! I was afraid to shout a warning – it might have startled you.' The expression on his face checked my natural impulse to laugh at his fears. As the others came straggling up he added in a matter-of-fact tone, 'If you had gone over I should have gone after you.' In the moment left to us we looked at one another in silence. We each knew that it was the key-note of our lives — where one went the other would go — to the mouth of hell or elsewhere — it didn't matter.

⁂

Well, I had plenty to distract my thoughts. A post had been offered me in Kensington, through the recommendation of Miss Buss. An ardent old North Londoner, a Miss Bennett, was starting a new school, and wanted to run it on the lines of the North London. Much to our satisfaction the post was non-resident, so that Mother and I could live together. The address of the school was West Kensington, of which we had never heard. We concluded that it must be even more aristocratic than Kensington, but were soon undeceived on this point. Aunt Lizzie had been very good in finding some rooms for us close to the school. At a turn in North End Road was a large public house called 'The Cedars', and opposite this was a row of good shops. One of these, a green-grocer's, was to be our new home. We didn't have to push through the greens and potatoes, but went up to our first-floor rooms by a private entrance. Mother was perfectly contented wherever you put her down. She always maintained that it was the people you lived with that mattered, and not the place. She at once admired the spacious sitting-room, and exclaimed, 'Look at the good view we get, in two directions, and with such a lot going on.' What entertained us both, and every one who came to see us, was the wall decoration. Not the usual romantic engravings, but huge oil-paintings in heavy gilt frames. Our landlady had lived in Spain and had brought them back with her, and that seemed to account for them amply. She said they were very old masters. They were certainly obscure from dirt and age, and this was greatly to their advantage, for it lent a mellowness and respectability to scenes that were mostly bloodthirsty or crude in their morality. One was a realistic rendering of something from the story of Susannah and the Elders, and another was the figure of Judith pacing home in quiet triumph, swinging the head of Holofernes, all dripping with blood, as though she had just picked it up cheap in the market, and cared not who knew it.

The scheme of colouring in the furniture was in harmony: carpet a fierce green, tablecloth a yellower green; chairs covered with crimson velvet, and some antimacassars of vermilion; but all were faded sufficiently to provide a quiet gaiety to the room as a whole.

The new school was only at five minutes' distance. Everything in it was beautifully arranged, but for the first few weeks there were only three pupils, so my labours were light. I had time to go on with my work for a degree, and have long tramps with Mother. She on her part did a good deal of exploring of the neighbourhood. When I came in to dinner on the second day she said 'We are in the odour of sanctity here. I have discovered that Burne-Jones has his studio just at the back of us. I saw his name on the door. And our landlady tells me that his famous briar-rose is in the garden.' It was not till later on that we heard the more interesting item about his house — that it was the home of Richardson at one time, and that he wrote *Pamela* there.

As soon as we were settled Mother wrote to Mr Hughes to suggest that he should come up to spend a Sunday with us, and as October 2nd was a Sunday and our common birthday, it seemed a good excuse for a little celebration, 'especially as Molly is to be twenty-one'. He replied that he could spend the Saturday night with his old friend Bourne, living in Camberwell, and would come on to us in time for midday dinner, and added that he was to be thirty.

Mother ordered roast fowl and its appurtenances — always a sign of festivity with her. We children used to say that she said grace more fervently over roast fowl than over roast mutton. When it came to the time for starting to church she announced that she was going to sample something fresh, as the church round the corner was so unstimulating; she had a mind to try the Roman Catholic Pro-cathedral; it sounded dignified anyhow. 'You can stop at home, dear, to receive Mr Hughes; I've been in the oven myself.' This was a reference to an old story about a girl who had disappeared; she could nowhere be found until a neighbour came in and suggested looking in the big brick oven; and there she was. When the neighbour was asked how she had guessed the hiding-place she said, 'I've been in the oven myself'.

So I was left at home alone, to await his arrival. A long time passed and the usual Sunday-morning lethargy was pervading North End Road. I gave up looking out of the window, for the traffic was hardly more than an occasional milk cart. I tried to read, but the words made no impression on my brain. Then I began to think that he had been unable to come after all . . . or that he had found his friend Bourne too engrossing . . . or that he had changed his mind and preferred to keep away . . . or that he had met with an accident . . . It was past twelve, and soon the landlady would be bustling in to lay the cloth for dinner, and then Mother would be returning. I was just thinking that I didn't care what happened if only something would happen, when I heard a hansom draw up outside. 'It isn't at our door,' I said to myself. 'Just go on with your book.' In another minute there were steps on the stairs, the door was thrown open, and the landlady announced 'Mr Hughes'. If she was listening at the door after closing it she must have been disappointed and no doubt surprised, for it was some time before a word was said. He stalked in, threw his hat down, took me in his arms and kissed me as if it were the natural salute.

It may be hard to believe (my three sons have difficulty in doing so), but this was the first kiss, other than fraternal, that I had ever experienced from a man of my own age. Perhaps I had missed a lot of enjoyment, but no amount of it could possibly have equalled the satisfaction of that first one. A bit unnerved, I felt that the silence must be broken somehow, and by something matter-of-fact. 'Won't you take your overcoat off?' I managed to say. No reply. Then I heard myself saying, 'Will it take off?' Even this absurdity did not strike either of us at the moment, and Mother returned while we were still standing bemused.

Dinner time passed off quite gaily, for Mother gallantly described her peculiar experiences at the Pro-cathedral with great gusto, and when we sat round the fire afterwards we were all talking naturally enough. We laughed over Arthur's attempts to see more of me in Cornwall. He had been so kindly entertained that he hadn't had a minute to himself, let alone a chance to walk up to Camborne. To get such a chance one day he announced that he had to send a telegram, and must go up to Camborne at once about it. Immediately a kindly cousin had offered to take it, as he was then going up to the town himself, and Arthur had been obliged to lay out a shilling on telling his mother that all was going well. Mother was merely amused at our difficulties in seeing one another. 'Those little obstacles', said she, 'merely enhance the pleasure of your meeting. One kiss behind the door is worth ten in front of it.' But, as Arthur pointed out, we hadn't managed to get even the stolen one. She was as enthusiastic about everything as we could wish, and with her unerring instinct for saying the right thing she announced firmly:

'You poor fools! You fancy yourselves in love with one another! Wait till ten years have passed, and then you will see how paltry this will seem compared to your love for one another *then*.'

By some blessed Dispensation of the Law, as inscrutable as providence, Gray's Inn required Arthur to dine there twice every fortnight. He used to get off on Saturday afternoon, eat one dinner, spend the night and Sunday morning at North End Road, and eat the second dinner before returning to Bedford. In order to have as long time with him as possible, I used to meet him at

*The Visit, by George Clausen*

St Pancras, and we would often do a picture gallery, or the like, before joining Mother at tea.

Time never hung heavy between these visits. Mother was continually discovering fresh interests in the neighbourhood, and new walks into 'almost country'. Friends and relations, mostly Cornish, were pretty frequent, and we could always have a spare room to put any one up. The mere fact of our living 'over a shop' was an attraction in itself, and Mary Wood was not the only one to be disappointed at not having to 'wade through onions to a throne', as she expressed it . . .

On one of his visits we had news for him. Barnholt was coming home for a short holiday. Good luck seemed to rain on us, for a glimpse of Barnholt was quite literally a rare treat. His letters were laughably laconic. Here is one that I happen to have kept:

> *Dear mother, I hope you are all right. We are just*
> *making Iquique. Give my love to little Molly.*
> *Your loving son Barnholt.*

But his presence was another matter, for he was the prime favourite with each of us, and we all rallied round. Of course he was to stay at North End Road, but Dym met him at Plymouth to bring him on. Tom came from Middlesbrough for a few days, and Arthur put in a short visit before going to Wales for Christmas. Those whom we couldn't accommodate put up at 'The Cedars'. Barnholt was hugely tickled at the greengrocer's shop, and greatly appreciated the variety of vegetables which our landlady served up every day as 'surprises' for us. One evening was specially gay, when Mr Bourne joined us and contributed his subacid wit to the conversation. The feast itself was simple, 'on a bottled beer footing', but at the close Mother unveiled a bottle of special sloe-gin that had come from Tony. Barnholt had been pouring forth the most exciting yarns, with the straightest face, and extreme economy of words. The sloe-gin reminded him of a man he met in an hotel in Valparaiso, who was talking very big about taste in wines. 'I'm glad to meet you,' said Barnholt, 'for I happen to have in my possession three bottles of a rare liqueur, of extremely delicate flavour, too good for ordinary people, really crying out for a man like you to taste it. I obtained it (don't ask me how) from the cellars of the King of Spain. If you like I'll go up to my room and bring you a specimen to try.' The man was interested, and proclaimed the pure water that Barnholt brought to him in a liqueur glass to be of the most delicate bouquet he had ever come across. He offered large money for the three bottles, or even for one, but nothing would induce Barnholt to part with them.

'That's right, Barney,' was Tom's comment, 'a true humorist never spoils his joke by telling a man how he has been fooled.'

Barnholt was as pleased with Arthur as the others were, but told me that he thought it was all nonsense for me to go on working for a degree.

'You see, Barney,' said I, 'we can't be married for some time, and to go on working at something hard is just the best thing for me, and really it's rather fun.'

'Right. But don't work too hard. Learn to knock off properly when you do knock off. Some people don't know how to be lazy. It's an art.'

*Advertisement for Beetham's Emollient Milk*

# 18

# EASTER AT ELSTOW, 1890

HERE does a decade end? This is a story of the eighties, and perhaps should end with the winter of 1889. But a compromise will suit me best, for the early part of 1890 brought such a change in my work and life that a full stop seems natural. As soon as the autumn term was over Mother and I put out for Cornwall. We were so anxious to arrive at Paddington in time that we started absurdly early, only to find that the winter time-table was different from the summer one, and that we had an hour and a half to wait. But Mother thought there were few things more amusing than a railway station when oneself was calm and other people were not. But one can be too calm. Dym met us as usual at Plymouth, and took us off for a cup of tea in Mill Bay station, where the refreshment-room was away from the platforms. We had heaps to talk and laugh about, and Dym assured us that there was no hurry, for refreshment-room clocks are kept fast, but when we thought it was about time we were taking our seats again, we found an empty platform and the red lights of the last train to Cornwall just disappearing. There was nothing to do but laugh, incriminate one another, send a telegram to uncle Joe, and go to an hotel. Now it is just possible that Mother's bed was damp – one seizes on any explanation, but ever after that holiday she was subject every now and again to mysterious pains. She would be perfectly well for a week or two, and able to take her long walks, and go sketching when it was fine; so that we hoped the trouble was passing off. When Easter was close at hand Arthur and I planned a special little holiday for her. I suppose we owe it to Moses, or perhaps some ancient moon-worshipper, that schools break up at different times in the spring. It chanced in '90 that my school was dispersed a full week before the one at Bedford; so Arthur suggested that Mother and I should take rooms for that week at the Swan Inn at Elstow, where he could come over to see us every day; and he hoped to get his friend Bourne for a day or two.

In those days the town had not encroached on Elstow, and the little village was one of those lovely spots of beauty that people are now beginning to value and try to 'preserve'. In addition to the usual beauties of old timbered cottages and thatched barns, great trees and a vivid, velvety 'green', it had an ancient moot-house, and a church with the curiosity of a tower separate from the main building. The association with Bunyan was another great attraction, and I liked to picture the jolly tinker drinking in the bar of the 'Swan' in his unregenerate days. Mother and I were entranced with the old inn itself, its rickety stairs and uneven floors, the homeliness of the innkeeper and his wife, the generous meals, and the one decoration on the wall of our sitting-room – a faded sepia print of biblical history from Adam and Eve to Revelation. I caught Mother and Arthur laughing quietly together one day over an episode in this print, which had been depicted with more vigour than delicacy, and I heard her say, 'Believe me, it's always the woman who does the tempting'. I was rather shocked at the time, but have since come to pretty much the same conclusion.

Everything combined to make that a happy week for Mother. She was in surroundings that recalled her boy Charles continually; she had recently had a letter from Barnholt who was expecting to come home in the summer; we had daily visits from Arthur and his fellow masters; and the weather was April at its best.

*Molly's mother, about 1850*

# 19

# I CUT THE PAINTER

O N the lovely May-day morning of 1890 my mother died, after an illness of only a few days. Nothing was here for tears: she had had a remarkably full and exhilarating life; she had an inborn capacity for casting care aside; she had always wished for a sudden death; and when she knew it to be at hand her only request was that I should be good to her sister Tony.

Now it was to this beloved Cornish aunt of mine that I owed, almost as much as to my parents, the two best gifts that any elders can bestow on any children – a happy childhood and as good an education as lies in their power. So that 'being good to Tony' involved no burden, but only continuing the delight of regarding her as a second mother, and spending part of every holiday with her in Cornwall.

And my mother left me wealthy. In money, no. It was a case of no work, no dinner. But I was young, healthy, and doing what I enjoyed. I was teaching in a girls' day-school in Kensington, under a fine headmistress, who allowed me to work along the lines I liked. Also I had three elder brothers, of whom I could never determine which was the most loved. Unfortunately, they were not at hand; the eldest, Tom, was living in Yorkshire with wife and children; the second, Dym, was more mobile as a bachelor, and was teaching mathematics in a school in Plymouth (a place on the way to Cornwall!); and the third, Barnholt, was at sea. These three would be bulwarks for me all through life, as Mother was well aware, but she had been accustomed to ejaculate occasion-ally, 'If only I saw you married to a good man I should die happy'. Well, she died quite at rest on that point, for on my twenty-first birthday I had become engaged to the man of all others that she admired most. This was Arthur Hughes, who, like Dym, was teaching mathematics. But, unlike Dym, he hated the work, and was reading for the Bar, not as an escape, but because the Law, even in its seemingly absurd intricacies, fascinated him. His work was at Bedford, and I saw something of him once a fortnight when he came up to Gray's Inn to 'eat his dinners'.

In spite of all these sources of wealth, I was desolate. A mother's death must always make one feel cut away at the roots, and in my case it was worse, because she had always been like a sister as well as a mother in her complete comradeship and youthful outlook. My brother Dym, whom she and I used to call 'the branch of our family at Plymouth', was well aware how badly I felt her loss, and came to the rescue by frequent letters and an occasional dash up to Kensington, to see me and take me out somewhere. As soon as the summer term was over he insisted on my spending a week with him on Dartmoor, where he and his friend Barber were as usual to be trout-fishing. He met me at Newton Abbot and took me on to Totnes for a day or two, where we could have some walks beside the broad waters of the Dart. I enjoyed the scenery and the walks enormously, but what bothered Dym was that I had no appetite, even after a long walk. I was really sorry about this, for he tried to tempt me with all he could think of. I remember his astonished cry, 'What! Not eat this salmon! Why, my dear child, it was in the Dart a few hours ago!' 'Oh, Dym,' I pleaded, 'I really would if I could.' 'Well, darling,' said he, 'we'll see what a drive over the moor will do for you tomorrow.'

The air on that glorious drive blew away my lassitude. I took off my hat and let the wind do what it liked with my close-cropped hair. I laughed as I hadn't laughed for many weeks, from sheer physical exhilaration, and I felt like a newly created being as we drew up at the Duchy Hotel, Princetown. Dym had mentioned our destination, and both town and hotel sounded very grand to me. Indeed I felt a little nervous about the small size of my bag, at which Dym had raised an eyebrow when he met me at Newton Abbot. But I was reassured on our arrival, for of town I saw none at all, and the hotel was surprisingly modest in appearance. To Dym it had become, from his frequent holidays spent there, almost a second home, and the proprietress welcomed us warmly. I soon found that the simplicity of the hotel was entirely confined to the things that didn't matter – its architecture and interior furnishings. Bedrooms and sitting-rooms were bare and even ugly, but the ducal quality of the hotel shone forth in its meals. These quite staggered me in their munificence. But I was prepared to justify them. How Dym laughed as he watched me dealing with the dinner after our arrival. The wind and sun of the moor had burnt my cheeks and sharpened my appetite to a quite inelegant extent; and not only Barber and his wife, but the other visitors too, couldn't help smiling. For this was one of those rare hotels (so rare that in a wide experience I have never come across another) where English people look cheerfully at all their fellow guests, and speak on the slightest provocation or none.

The meals were peculiar in another way. They faded out in the middle of the day. In fact the whole hotel faded out. After giving us a colossal breakfast, including real ham, fish, new-laid eggs, chops and steaks, raspberries and bilberries, and bowls of clotted cream at decent intervals on the table, the entire staff disappeared. I imagined that they went into contemplation on the subject of evening dinner for some hours, and then it was all hands to the task of creating it. Such degrading trifles as lunch and tea were nothing accounted of. Mrs Barber and I were the only female guests, and the men were all there for outdoor sport of some kind. I don't know about the others, but Dym used to go the whole day between breakfast and dinner without opening his mouth, either to put anything in or utter a word. He and Barber would set off for the stream, the upper reaches of the Dart, lost to everything except trout, for they designedly fished well apart so as not to interfere with each other's sport.

Meanwhile, Mrs Barber and I knew our role quite well: we had the freedom of the moor, but must on no account come near the fishermen lest we disturb the trout, who (so the men asserted) had a rooted objection to womenfolk. Not far from the hotel was a tiny shop, the village Whiteley we called it, for it was so full of oddments of universal provision that it was difficult to edge into it. Indeed, there was a little home-made notice pinned by the door, 'Please enter sideways'. We suspected that this had been put there by some wag in the hotel. Here we would capture every morning a few biscuits or apples or nuts to take with us on our wanderings about the moor. We also took books, but I read very little, liking rather to bask in the sun and give myself up to the uncanny fascination of the boundless moor. The time passed rapidly, and we didn't even pine for a cup of tea at four o'clock, but weren't we all ready for our evening dinner!

*By 1891 Molly was tired of her residential post at Miss Bennett's school in Kensington. She had taken her B.A. when she was offered the newly-created post of training teachers at Bedford College. With Miss Rogers, a fellow student from Cambridge days, she moved into the Ladies' Residential Chambers. Arthur had been called to the Bar and was also living in London, starting out on his legal career.*

Arthur had taken temporary lodgings in Great Coram Street, sinister in

*Harvest Time on the Dart, by Edmund George Warren*

sound and appearance. I do not care to let my fancy roam over his diet during this period. He told me that an aggressively successful barrister said to him one day, 'Ah, Hughes, what do you do, ah, about lunch?' 'Oh, that's simple enough,' replied Arthur, 'if I have any money I have lunch, and if not I don't.'

His first case in Court was an excitement for both of us. I had a telegram with the single word 'Won', and on the following evening went with him and his solicitor to the pantomime. The choice of entertainment lay with the solicitor who bought the seats, and we managed to conceal our boredom through the whole show – transformation scene, clown-tricks, and everything.

Soon after this he managed to get quarters in Gray's Inn, some delightful old oak-panelled rooms in Field Court, in a building subsequently pulled down. Indeed it was in a shaky condition even then. But how lovely the flavour of the rooms and how easily they were comfortably furnished with two deep basket chairs, a second-hand table, and two of Charles's pictures on the walls. And the big windows looked out on Gray's Inn Gardens, with the cawing of rooks and memories of Bacon. Arthur was 'done for' by his laundress, Mrs Keyes, one of the most lovable women I have ever met. Rosy-cheeked, of uncertain age, invariably bonneted, she appeared to rejoice in her work, which was mostly confined to cooking breakfast on a small gas-stove, and tidying up generally. I asked Arthur why she was called a 'laundress', and he said that the usually accepted theory was that laundresses were so called because they never washed anything. What she enjoyed most was the arrival of visitors. And of these there was no lack. The brothers of the family, 'the boys' as I always called them, were the most frequent visitors. The parson brother, Llewelyn, used to like an excuse to run up to town to see that the bishops were doing their duty at some Assembly or other. The doctor brother, Alfred, was now professor of anatomy at Cardiff, and very well off, and couldn't keep away from London for long. My own brothers, Tom and Dym, were equally bitten with the love of the old town, and could always be sure of a hearty welcome and a shake-down in the ample rooms in Field Court. Of course no casual visitor ever invaded Arthur's sacred room in the Temple, complete with law-books and clerk.

In the spring of '93 the best visitor of all arrived. My sailor brother Barnholt had three weeks' leave. This he parcelled out between us. Dym met him at Plymouth and kept him for the first week, then he went to Tom in Yorkshire for the second week, and the last week he spent in Gray's Inn. Tom and Dym stole a weekend from their work to run up to town, anxious to have every possible moment with their favourite brother. I used to go over to tea, to 'pour out' for them all, and enjoy the endless talk, and be chaffed and teased as in the old days at home in Canonbury. Two or three times Barnholt ventured to the Ladies' Residential Chambers, to see that I was all right. He was a bit overawed by Miss Rogers, who was extremely large, and he insisted on giving her what she called the brevet title of *Mrs* Rogers. She took the liveliest interest in all the boys, and especially in Arthur. As for herself, she had a most charming mother who used to come to see us now and again, but of love-story she had none. She told me that at the age of sixteen she looked in her mirror and said, 'You are very plain; make up your mind once for all that no one will ever want to marry you.' There seemed to me more heroism and pathos in this than in lots of novels, for instead of being soured by her unattractive appearance she was full of wit and humour and warm-heartedness. She was fond of what she called the 'three-volume' story of the Devon maiden: 'the first time she married was because she was young and silly-like; the second time she married it was for cows and sich; but the third time she married it was for pure, pure *lov*.'

During the few hours that Barnholt spent in Gray's Inn when Arthur and the others were not there, he was fully entertained by Mrs Keyes. She dusted the room over and over again while he regaled her with yarns of dreadful storms 'round the Horn' in a sailing vessel, with the sailors on their knees in despair. And she had quite as harrowing disclosures to make of horrors in Gray's Inn.

'Down below, 'ere, Sir, in these 'ere very buildings, there's corpses.'

She had been during one spell of her lurid career a kitchen-hand in a London restaurant, and had seen things.

'Don't you never eat in no restaurant, Sir. Me and Keyes could tell you things . . . what they does to make the vegetables green! and the thick soup! Ah!'

The dear soul broke down with genuine grief when the news came, some two months later, of Barnholt's death in South America.

*The Law Courts, by Joseph Pennell*

# 20

# AMERICA CALLING

THE long vacation of '93 was close at hand, and Cornwall in my mind's eye, when I had a surprise. I had been selected to represent Bedford College at Chicago. The 'World's Fair' was being held there, a huge exhibition of everything, outshining our London 'Fisheries', Naval Exhibition, and such-like. In connection with it, as a kind of serious sideshow, was a big Educational Conference. My duties were to be simple, merely to attend any meetings that seemed useful, to read at one of them a paper by Mrs Bryant, and to write a report when I returned. Expenses were to be paid, and there was nothing to prevent my going. My natural advisers, Arthur, Dym, and Tony, were all for my seizing such a chance. They had all travelled abroad and knew the value of seeing strange places, and I had seen nothing more foreign than Wales and Cornwall; and as for a sea voyage, the only steamboat I had experienced was a penny paddle-boat on the Thames.

The eight of us who had been chosen from various schools and colleges met at a house in Gower Street, to be introduced to each other and to receive final instructions and books of tickets from Mrs Henry Fawcett. For travel on board ship she told us that the most useful thing was a hold-all, about a foot and a half square, made of brown holland, and endowed with pockets of different sizes, to contain slippers, brush and comb, handkerchiefs, and so on. It could be rolled up with a strap, and made to carry odds and ends. With this and a cabin-trunk we should be complete. I bought the cabin-trunk with comparative ease, but spent several feverish hours of the short time left in concocting, with the help of Miss Rogers, this confounded hold-all. It caused Arthur much amusement, but beyond this it had no advantages. Seldom was anything in its right pocket, no article was really held and the whole contraption (intended to be hung by tapes in the cabin) was never within reach when wanted.

Arthur arranged a pleasant treat for the evening before I was to start, a concert at the Albert Hall, to hear Patti (her 'positively last appearance'). London was gay with flags and flowers and illuminations, to celebrate the royal wedding, and the initials G and M were everywhere. All I remember of the concert was the glorious voice of Patti, and the thrill that ran through the audience at her encore when the first notes of 'Home Sweet Home' reached us. I can still hear the long-drawn beauty of the word 'home' as she filled the vast hall with it, and the thunder of applause when the song closed.

The following evening Arthur came to put me and my belongings on a cab and see me off by the night train for Liverpool. 'I've put in my pocket,' said he, 'a small flask of brandy for you to put in that hold-all, because you never know.' Trying to be funny at Euston I asked an official which was the platform for New York. 'Number 15. Change at Liverpool' was the reply immediately snapped out at me. Arthur was full of anxieties and final instructions, and it was not until the train was gathering speed that I realized that he had forgotten to give me his flask. On arrival at Liverpool I fell in with the three educational delegates who were to travel with me. No city is at its best at six o'clock in the morning, and after a prowl round the streets until it was possible to get an hotel breakfast, we felt that we had sucked the pleasures of Liverpool dry, and were glad to go aboard.

Our boat was the *Adriatic*, never one of the latest type of ocean greyhound, I imagine, and now nearing its age for retirement. But to me it seemed both spacious and amusing. We were travelling second class and had a cabin between the four of us, and much happy time was consumed in arranging our luggage and exploring the vessel. Why this awkward wooden bar at the entrance to our cabin I asked, why little holders for the glasses, how do I get up into my berth, do we all wash out of this basin? As soon as we started all other interests were sunk in the delight of watching the sea, but towards late afternoon I began to be what Jane Austen calls 'a little disordered', climbed up to my top berth, and didn't feel like climbing down again.

That was the first day. We were told that the voyage would take ten days, but they seemed like a hundred. I envied my companions who were able to get up, have meals, go on deck, and apparently enjoy themselves, and I sucked what amusement I could from watching their oddities. One slept extremely well and snored unfailingly. Another was of a literary turn and begged us not to gaze on her Dianic form while she washed. The third seemed to have an obsession about her belongings and was always rearranging her luggage. When they had gone up on deck I had the cabin to myself for the bulk of the day. It was then that I suffered from claustrophobia, in addition to my nausea. The top of our cabin was only about a foot above my head – quite bearable at night, but incredibly oppressive all day long. After a struggle down for a wash, up again I would climb, and get some distraction from 'noises without'. These

*'Goodbye' on the Mersey, by J.J.J. Tissot*

consisted chiefly of the sounds of people hurrying to and fro, and I guessed that we must be between the dining-room and the kitchen, for amid the medley of shouting, snatches of popular songs, and the clash of washing-up, I discerned orders for food: 'Irish stew for a lady' (was this a small portion?) 'Dry 'ash four times.' I tried to picture what dry 'ash could possibly be, but am ignorant to this day; Arthur saw it on a restaurant menu some months later, and ordered it so that he might tell me, but said that he would rather not refer to the subject again. At night the sound of scrubbing predominated, except during one period of the voyage when the fog-horn drowned all music but its own. I rather liked this, for it suggested the possibility of a collision when the roof of the cabin might be broken. The stewardess was a cheerful body who said 'Yus' to everything, and I suppose she must have brought me something to swallow now and again. She assured me that I should be well by Wednesday, because people always were. Wednesday came and went, and I still lay there thinking of the riddle of my childhood that compared the *Adriatic* to a dry attic. I thought too of the rich man's reply to his steward's 'What can I fetch you, Sir?' – 'Fetch me an island.' I could raise a laugh over this, for I remembered from geography lessons that the good old Atlantic was five miles deep.

One afternoon as I lay there, going over such silly ideas and shutting my eyes against that terrible ceiling, I felt the unmistakable touch of a man's hand, laid, large and gentle, on mine. Turning my head I opened my eyes on a tall and kindly looking man in uniform.

'Who are you?' I asked, smiling with pleasure at any break to my thoughts.

'I'm the ship's doctor,' said he, 'and you must try to come up on deck, or you will be really ill.'

*On Deck*

Cheered by his mere manner I struggled into some clothes and found some one to help me along the passages and up on to the deck again. How lovely was the fresh air and the sight of the sea, and the sound of the talk of the others. They welcomed me heartily, one wrapped a rug round me and another brought me a tot of brandy, and I knew then for the first time the magic effect of this godsend of a restorative. Time didn't hang so heavily now, but I think that Columbus himself was not more pleased at a sight of America than I to have Long Island pointed out to me, to see fireworks ashore and the varied lights of the shipping that we were passing. Sickness left me and I even made my way into the dining-room and ordered something to eat.

We docked early in the morning, and my first contact with America was the big customs-shed of New York. The officials were tall and leisurely, always sucking something and completely indifferent to any one's concerns. It gave me an absurd shock to hear them talking English quite easily, and me having come all that way! The four of us who had shared a cabin kept together for mutual protection, and ventured forth into the streets. They seemed much like those at home, only far noisier. We tried a little restaurant for lunch, and greatly amused the people by our ignorance of the strange coinage. Refreshed, we began to look about, and presently one of us discovered through some advertisement that it was possible to go to Washington by train. We knew that Washington was the capital, but it seemed a long way off, and we had no notion that trains were common enough in America for people to go about casually as we did in England.

'But what about Chicago?' I demurred. 'We have to get there somehow, and Cook's man has told us how to.'

'Oh, but there's sure to be some kind of railway-line to get there from Washington,' argued the bolder spirit, 'and we may never in our lives have the chance to see Washington if we don't now. Oh do let's.'

So we all went to the station, after learning to our amusement that we must never ask for the 'station' (a very different place), but for the 'depot'. Here we found ourselves among a large number of passengers, just like one sees at Liverpool Street Station on any Saturday afternoon. Only in New York there was no agitated speculation as to which platform or what hour. Every one was seated comfortably in an airy waiting-room until the summons came for the train. 'Why can't we go on the platform,' I wondered. I soon saw the reason. There was no platform. We had to step up into the train from the line, or 'track' as they called it. Here were fresh surprises for us. Instead of the stuffy little upholstered compartments on our English railways (where people never agree as to how much fresh air may be let in) there were spacious, long, open carriages, where we could move about in comfort, change our seats so as to get different points of view, arrange our belongings, and make frequent excursions to the end of the car where iced water was provided free! We had hardly started when white-coated boys came along, proclaiming for sale all sorts of little luxuries – magazines, fans, tempting fruit, candy . . . . When I exclaimed that it seemed to me a kind of fairyland, one of our party argued that it was all very well for the Americans to have all these modern improvements, but it was the English who had started railways, and had to work off the old stock. I was obliged to concede this point, but felt more sympathy with her next remark about the views from the windows, which compared unfavourably enough with our English countryside: she said that her respect for the Pilgrim Fathers was much increased, for they must have been extremely earnest about their religion to leave England for America. I wished we could have seen more of Philadelphia than we managed to spy from the railway, for Penn had always been one of my heroes.

However, Washington made up for all and exceeded my best expectations. In mid-July this lovely city was hotter than anything I had ever experienced, but was a dream of delight. White and green were the prevailing tones, from beautiful houses and huge trees. Spacious streets were being continually watered with great splashing hoses that made our little lumbering water-carts seem funny in comparison. There were few people about at that time of year, and our hotel was nearly empty, and hardly any attendants to be seen. After consulting with one another we rang for the chambermaid, and a Negro appeared! But he was quite efficient for all we wanted. My chief need was a bath, and I never enjoyed one so much before or since. Then a real bed to lie down in. My first night in America will never fade from my memory.

We were up early the next morning to make the most of the few hours before we were to start for Chicago. The Capitol astounded us; we had no idea that the Americans knew how to build anything so large and impressive. But we were far more fascinated by the White House, a homely looking villa so near the roadway that we felt inclined to tap on the window and ask how they were getting on.

How silent and dignified the city seemed on that Sunday afternoon as we made our way to the depot to get our train for Chicago. But here we came upon a new phase of American life. The depot was all a-bustle with Negroes starting on excursions. Believe me, I had always pictured Negroes, if not naked, attired in the minimum, or in white garments of some slight kind. Here they were outdoing our 'Ampstead 'Arries and 'Arriets in the colour and extravagant splendour of their holiday clothes. I had a chat with a woman who was carrying a real live black baby in a snow-white dress. She was pleased at my admiring the little fellow, and let me hold him a bit. I was sorry to leave Washington.

Our first point of excitement on the journey was Harper's Ferry. This romantic spot actually existed, and there we were, passing through it quite casually. Our enthusiasm amused our fellow passengers, some of whom appeared to know less about John Brown than we did. I was struck with the extreme readiness of these people to talk to us and start a temporary friendship. My own family had always been inclined to chat with a traveller at any time, but our chattiness was cool reserve compared to that of Americans. At first I was a little on the defensive, but soon began to enjoy and appreciate this general friendliness. After all it's the best way to 'see' a country, and get various opinions and meet new people; and there was the ever-blessed link of a common language. A common language, yes, but every one spotted us as English. 'How do you know I'm English?' I asked a pleasant sea-captain who begged to join us at our tea in the 'parlour car', and entertained us with yarns from a world-wide experience. His reply was immediate: 'By your way of talking and by your bright complexion.' It was news to me that I had either.

When dusk fell our Negro porter came to make up our couches for the night. Now I had not been anything but hot since leaving New York, and I besought him not to pile on the rugs. 'You're hot now,' said he, 'but wait till we are going over the Alleghanies, and see if you don't pull them round you.' I lay down and enjoyed the quiet evening effect as the sun was setting over the hills, and then there came over me that odd feeling (that has always attacked me at intervals) of being alone in the world, and I began to wonder what on earth I was doing careering over a strange continent. Not for long; the Negro was right; the night grew cold, and rolling myself up in my rugs I fell happily asleep.

In the morning we managed to have a sketchy kind of wash in the train. It was badly needed, for the soot on a railway journey in America was like nothing we get in England. Great lumps of soot nestled into our clothes. Our captain explained it as due to the softness of the coal, so nothing could be done about it. We were indeed sorry to say good-bye to this Captain Riley, who was going on, while we had to change for Chicago. We talked eagerly of the meal we intended to have at the junction, picturing a kind of Bristol refreshment room, for the tea in the 'parlour car' had not been very sustaining, and it was now eight o'clock in the morning. But Cincinnati Junction turned out to be no

*Passengers Dining in a Pullman Railway Car*

more than a wooden track, with a small shed on it. This shed was evidently a refreshment-room, but all that was left to eat consisted of two buns on a glass dish. 'How much are these buns?' said I to the woman presiding over them. Staring at me she exclaimed in rich nasal twang, 'How funny you do talk!' When I laughed and said that we had come from an outlandish place called England, she said we could have the buns for nothing (although she called them by some other word which I forget). These didn't go far to stay the hunger of the four of us, and as we were wondering rather dismally where and when our next meal would be, in came the Chicago express. We had hardly taken our seats when a white-robed waiter stalked along the train, proclaiming in each car the joyful news: 'Breakfast is served in the rear car.' Course after course was placed before us, including fruit, porridge and cream, omelettes, fish and cutlets. We enjoyed as much as the swaying of the train allowed us to convey to our mouths, and with much laughter we agreed that the waiter deserved a good tip, although the price of the breakfast itself was a bit staggering. I said that I had plenty of change and would see to the tip. A shilling seemed to me handsome enough, and I left on the table what I took to be a shilling, but I noticed as we were leaving the car that the waiter looked anything but pleased, and it was not till several hours later that I realized the value of the nickel I had so generously given him.

We felt that another meal in that train was beyond our means, and arrived at Chicago at about 6.30 in the evening, very tired, dirty, and hungry. Different places for boarding had been assigned to us, so our foursome party was split up. Two of us were to be lodged at the University, and looked forward with confidence to an immediate and pleasant reception. We pictured the University as a dignified cluster of colleges in some prominent part of the town, as well known to the inhabitants as King's is to Cambridge people. Having been warned that cabmen were apt to be extortionate we thought to economize by taking the elevated railway, but there was no ready response when we asked for tickets to take us as near the University as possible. Each person consulted recommended a different station to aim at. So we tried one after another along the line, looking out in vain for anything that suggested a university. Back and forth we went, and it was now getting dark. One fellow traveller strongly recommended the Exhibition station, and although anything more unlike a university than an exhibition it was hard to imagine, we determined to get out and give the idea a trial. We started off walking along several unmade roads deep in dust, getting no nearer anywhere promising. I was wearing the slippers into which I had changed for the railway journey, and they were hardly the thing for a suburban walk in Chicago in the dark. Ploughing through one road I left a shoe stuck in the soil, and as I retrieved it I thought of Tadpole's similar accident and laughed. 'There's nothing to laugh at,' said my companion. 'We don't want to be out here all night, and there's not even a cab to be had in this region.' Just then I spied a kind of open café, with lights and people moving about. We went in and told them our plight. They were very kind and brought out a map of Chicago. Accustomed to the complexity of London, with its muddle but at least a few main streets, I was defeated by this chess-board of straight roads crossing one another at right angles and all apparently of equal importance, and numbered like convicts. But those in the know read it quite easily, and our good Samaritans soon found that the University was indeed close to the Exhibition. So we must have been circling round it all the time.

What with the soot of the railway and the dust of the streets we felt quite unfit for a dignified arrival at the University. We needn't have worried; there was a warm welcome for us from those who had already arrived and were getting anxious about us; there was a copious supper covered by netting to keep the flies off; various kinds of baths and bedrooms; and all troubles were soon drowned in sound sleep. Next morning I was quickly at my window to see my surroundings by daylight. When I saw the extremely new buildings and the wooden planks laid on the ground for people to walk from one to another, I began to see that the whole thing was still 'in the making', and to wonder no longer that the bulk of the people of Chicago had not yet heard of their university. After all, I reflected, even Oxford itself must have been new once, or at least parts of it now and then, like Keble; and I tried to picture what Chicago University would be like in a few thousand years.

I went down to breakfast and found the supper-room of the night before a noisy scramble of catch-as-catch-can. But there was plenty to eat and general camaraderie among the strangers from all quarters who were boarded in the University — some fifty in number. The Educational Congress was being held in a large building in another part of the town, and a party of us started off all business-like with note-books. I ran back to fetch something from my room and was shocked to find my bed being made by a Negro. It was not that he was a Negro, but that a man should be doing such a domestic and intimate job . . . a job that I used to do for my brothers, but the other way about seemed all wrong. When I breathed my discomfiture to the others they laughed and told me I should soon get used to it. But I never did, and kept well away when this menial task was due.

Our short daily journey was on the Illinois Central overhead railway. The little stations and carriages were all primitive and ramshackly; there were no doors at all to the compartments; we were kept in by a long iron bar which was worked by the guard: he would pull it back at each station for a few moments, for people to get in or out, and they had to nip about quickly for fear of being caught by the bar in transit. In principle it was like our modern sliding doors on the Tube, but how different in practice!

Any one who has ever looked in at an Educational Conference needs no description of it. The same uplifting speeches are delivered at them all, no doubt the same that bored the Athenians and drove the Romans to the Baths. Of the many that we endured at Chicago I have memories of only two: a rousing straight-from-the-shoulder, human address from Commissioner Harris; and the curious contrast of a paper read by the Russian Prince Sergius, whose deliberate style and old-world polish enchanted me. Most of the American speakers took themselves more seriously than English people do, and were correspondingly more wearisome. The real value of such conferences lies in the discussions in corridors and side-rooms, at lunches and teas, when teachers will confess to strangers what they really do do, where they have despaired, and where succeeded a bit. They recommend books to one another and pore together over the publishers' stalls. In Chicago these were good, and I made many casual friends while discussing and buying. Teachers had come from great distances and were obviously enjoying a good time, perhaps their best holiday for many years. I think Chaucer would find good scope today for more tales among these modern pilgrims, and instead of the old slogan 'St Thomas is the best doctor' we might have a new one – 'An Educational Conference is the best doctor' – for it gives teachers a change physically and mentally, if it is only to see the absurdity of their own solemnity.

Those few of us who were English graduates were referred to as *alumnae*, and were amused to find ourselves lionized and invited hither and thither. I actually spent a week-end at the home of a wealthy Chicago merchant, who had a 'place' on the lake-side. This was my one and only chance to be for longer than an hour or two inside a real American home, and it was quite unlike what I expected. The house was large and 'well appointed' in every way, but there was total lack of domestic service, even of 'coloured help'. Meals were on a big scale, but the mother cooked, and we all fetched what we wanted, cleared away, washed up, and so on, with great fun. This struck me as a far more satisfactory arrangement than one finds in some English households, where there is more service than things being served. My chief pleasure was in their only child, a little girl of four who did her best to get in the way of everybody and make me romp with her on the grand staircase.

One other example of American hospitality stands out in my memory. A Mrs Catsinger, of Austin, invited a few of us one afternoon to meet her husband and children, and some American *alumnae*. We didn't go into the house, but were entertained in a large garden, where quite a poetical meal was served as we 'sat around'. A full-sized English butler with his satellites brought salads and ices and most unusual little cakes of a dainty kind, as well as varied drinks. Conversation was at a high level, but not heavy or self-conscious; as an intellectual treat it was the best I had in Chicago.

As an extreme contrast to this I recall a visit to what was called a Chatauqua meeting, a kind of blend of education and religion. To these people the teaching of the young seemed to be too solemn and important to talk about calmly, and I was obliged to come away quite hurriedly.

Our two chief amusements, when the rigours of the conference were over for the day, were the Exhibition and shopping. To examine the shop-windows of a strange town is an unfailing source of recreation to a Londoner. I was puzzled by these in Chicago. Drapery was easy to find, but there appeared to be no simple bakers or grocers or chemists. I wanted some biscuits, and tried to describe them to a kindly shopkeeper. It is really harder to describe a biscuit than you would think. 'Oh,' he exclaimed at last, 'what you want is crackers.' 'No, no,' I protested, picturing the bon-bons of Christmas time. But he was right, and I learnt another American word. We should have spent more time in prowling about the city and watching people at work, if the streets had not been so filthy with spitting. No English person would believe how bad it was, requiring us to pick every step we took on the pavements in even the best streets. And in the trams it was far worse, because there was less accommodation for the disgusting habit. So we generally gravitated to the World's Fair, which was kept, by some unknown means, beautifully clean, in spite of the crowds of people. But cleanliness isn't everything, and I missed the tang of Chicago's reality. Just like conferences, all exhibitions and fairs are very much alike – grand white temporary palaces, artificial lake, lit by fairy lights, Javan and Indian villages (one native village was rather too realistic with its war-cries), Saratoga gold-mine, glass-blowing, gun-making, and a big Transportation building. The midway Plaisance afforded endless side-shows (including 'a peep at your future home' and a Congress of Beauty). Restaurants at every corner were convenient and tempting but ruinously expensive. A phonograph band produced a more hideous noise than any I had previously known. On the whole I preferred the dirty streets, but was certainly shocked at the river of Chicago, in which I think a spoon would easily have stood up.

So far as we could discover there was no important 'sight' in Chicago that visitors were supposed to 'do'. The only special thing that we had associated with the town was the pork factory, but we had been warned not on any account to visit the stock-yard, because the killing of the pigs was an insufferable sight. Of course we had heard that the organization was so complete that the pig walked in at one end and came out at the other in the form of sausages. Two of our party felt that such marvellous management must be well worth seeing, and really *ought* to be investigated, if Chicago was to be thoroughly visited. So they went to the office and explained to the man in charge that they wished to see something of the processes, but to avoid the actual scene of the killing. 'Sure,' said he, scenting no doubt that he had some elegant hypersensitive English ladies to deal with, and immediately he ushered them straight into the slaughter-house, where some thousand pigs were being dispatched. They rushed away and were really ill for a few hours. I had a sneaking sympathy with that man.

As soon as the conference was over our party was expected to return to England. Two of us, however, felt inclined to see some more of the continent, now we had come so far. We both had friends in Canada who had invited us to pay them a visit, and it was simply flying in the face of Providence not to go. My friend started off at once for Winnipeg, but I was only going as far as Toronto and was able to stay with the rest of our party a little longer. Our route was planned to give us a short stay at the Niagara Falls. I think we were all sorry to say good-bye to Chicago, where we had begun to feel at home, and started off on our night journey quite reluctantly. Early in the morning our train was halted to give the passengers a view of the Falls. This seemed to me extremely funny. In England one looked upon a train's business as serious — speed — getting there — that was the main consideration; the idea of stopping to look at a beauty spot was merely frivolous. Nor on reflection did I think it good policy if Americans wanted mere passers-by to see the Falls. From the train they were as disappointing as a first glimpse of Stonehenge seems to any one going by in a car. One has to come close to these monsters before one can feel the terrifying effect they must have had on the worshippers of the sun-god. And so with Niagara; it was only after we had been for an hour or two in an hotel overlooking the Falls and within the sound of their roar that their grandeur seized us. While we were strolling round, getting various points of view and looking down into the whirlpool in which Captain Webb lost his life, we discovered that it was possible (for the sum of two dollars) to go right under one of the Falls. Why boggle at two dollars, we thought, for such a glory?

Accordingly the three of us went into a little wooden cabin, stripped off all our clothes and got into mackintoshes provided for us. Then we went into a rather crazy-looking lift and were lowered to the base of the Fall. Here we stepped out and followed our guide. He led us over a stony way and soon we were right under the great cataract of water. The noise was now deafening. Although well accustomed to jumping from boulder to boulder on the Cornish shore, I found these slippery rocks far worse. We were not roped, and in the semi-darkness I was aware that the least mistake of a step would send one down into the ugly backwash of the river swirling round us. I lost my nerve and yelled to the guide to take us back, but the noise was so great that I might as well have yelled to the moon. Fortunately the others had not heard me either, and were sturdily following me. In fact there was no possible means of turning safely however much we had wanted to. So, facing up to the idea that any moment might be my last, I fixed my gaze on the guide's broad back and trod forward. What a relief it was to come out from the gloom and roar, and to be able to take hold of something wooden. There is something human and comforting in the touch of wood. Is this a relic of our simian past? On looking

*The Falls of Niagara, by Richard Wilson*

back on that expedition, however, I think that our next bit of walk was quite as crazy an undertaking as the struggle over the wet rocks. A series of planks was placed over the foot of the Fall, and provided with a hand-rail, and along this 'bridge' we made our way amid the foam back again to our lift. There was no room for thoughts of danger, for we were quite overcome with the beauty of the scene. We looked right up at the mass of falling water dazzling white in the sunshine, with an undertone of emerald. No view from the top could ever have come near it. When the hotel clerks and visitors heard where we had been they declared that nothing would induce them to go down. We felt quite distinguished, especially as we had been given certificates to show beyond doubt that we had actually gone under the Fall.

On the next day I parted from my original cabin companions—they were for New York and England, and I took ship for Toronto, where I was to be met by my Canadian host and hostess.

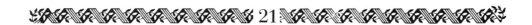 

# 21

# BOSTON, MASS.

*After her Canadian visit, Molly parted from an older English companion, who was 'full of compunction at leaving me alone on the continent. "Alone on the continent!" The idea went to my head like wine. I was free. I laughed on my way back to the hotel at the absurdity of having all America to play about in. For a first venture from England this seemed good.'*

WHILE parting so gaily from my fellow traveller I was hugging to myself a plan. I would spend a few days of those left before my boat was due to sail, in a visit to Boston.

My 'knowledge' of Canada had received continual rebuffs, but then it was a huge tract of country, whereas Boston was only one town, and I really did know a good deal about it. It was more familiar to English ears than New York itself. Called after the little seaport of Boston, Lincs., it had far outshone its godfather, and many a letter intended for England had gone over to Boston, Mass. The point that tickled me most was that Boston was 'not in America'. The ultra-exclusive inhabitants were neither English nor American, but just Bostonians – *sui generis*. I was eager to hear the special kind of accent they had developed. It was also a pleasure to know that the town could not be laid out in the chess-board style of Chicago. The streets were so narrow and in-and-out that a man had been known to catch his own coat-tails in hurrying round a corner. And yet the town must be modern and busy, for the legend ran that they killed a man a day in the traffic. Altogether a most alluring spot. If a bit medieval here and there, that was appropriate, because this Botolph's town had been named after a kindly East Anglian saint who protected travellers. Indeed, in old days a prayer and small donation to St Botolph were an insurance for your journey. I didn't appeal to him but to the next best thing to a saint, a kindly fellow guest at the hotel in Montreal. He recommended the route through the White Mountain district, and perhaps he was inspired by St

Botolph, for it was a heavenly journey from first to last.

Neither knowing nor caring how long the journey would be, I put into my hold-all a few things that experience had taught me might be handy as I went along, and checked my trunk to Boston. I wondered how my friend could ever have lost a package of any kind, since this system of checking was simplicity itself – you cared not how your luggage got on, nor what route it took – it was bound to find its fellow check in due course, and you had that in your pocket.

After an early start from Montreal there was a midday change at a place called Johnsburg (as well as I remember). Here was a chance for a refreshing wash, a sandwich, and a glass of milk. Apparently it was a border station, and when we started in the train that came up we were in the States. It is difficult to say why I was so pleased to be under the stars and stripes again; it seemed as vaguely attractive as being entirely by myself, I had to be neither submissive nor loyal. I now settled down for a good long run to Boston, put on slippers and travelling cap, and placed a book handy for reading, but found the scenery getting ever more interesting as the train wound among the hills. I was feeling at the acme of comfort, when by came the conductor to examine tickets. There were few passengers in the car, so he was in no hurry and seemed inclined for a chat.

'What time this evening do we reach Boston?' I asked.

'This evening! We shan't get there this evening at all.'

'A night in the train?' said I in dismay. 'Why, that will mean missing all this beautiful scenery.'

'Well, if that's what you want, why not spend the night somewhere on the way, and go on tomorrow by daylight?' Then pulling out his list of stations he added, 'Look here, Fabyans is a fine spot, and a good hotel there and all. I could put you ashore there.'

'Good hotel! But my trunk is checked on to Boston, and I've only this little hold-all. I can't possibly put up like this at a decent hotel.'

'Oh, don't you mind about clothes. They're all just holiday people there. You settle down again comfortably; I'll tell you when to get ready to jump out – about four o'clock.'

For the next two hours we ran through distractingly lovely country, all too fast, now through woods, now across wild moorland, now pushing a way through hedges so close that they brushed the windows; indeed at one time I thought we should be caught in the branches. And all around were hills. The sun was shining and fleecy clouds were throwing shadows in a way that reminded me of Wales.

*The Colonnade of a Large American Hotel*

Was there an hotel at Fabyans! There was nothing else. The railway station was its front door. I was the only passenger to get out. The train was off at once, and I had no choice but to go in. The word 'holiday-makers' had suggested a little wayside shanty, with the minimum of amenities, and people in camping outfit – and a couple of dollars the amount of the bill. To my surprise and distress I walked into a magnificent lounge, decorated expensively with ferns, flowers, flags, and festoons, as though for some gala occasion. A huge log fire was crackling in the grate, and rest-inviting chairs were scattered about. The many people talking and laughing about the place were of a type I had not seen before in America, obviously both wealthy and cultivated, all well dressed, but quite simply, and every one seemed carefree and jolly. How awkward I felt, standing in the entrance watching them – me with my ridiculous little hold-all and travel-stained clothes. Seeing a little office at one side I went up to the reception clerk, told him plainly my predicament, and holding out a gold piece said that I expected he would like to be paid in advance as I had no luggage. He was shocked at such an idea, and had me conducted at once to a dainty little room with a fine view of the hills. The chambermaid informed me that hot baths were always to be had, and meals were served continually in the dining-

*The North Country, by Willard Metcalf*

room, to suit the various holiday outings of the guests, and then she asked whether I wanted anything else.

I didn't tell her so, but my wants were many. I turned out my hold-all to see what could be done. In addition to the slippers and cap and small toilet necessities, there was little beyond the inevitable *Hamlet*, my sketching-book and paint-box, and the book I had bought to read in the train and neglected (*A Window in Thrums*). But fortunately I found in one of the pockets a needle-case, and was glad enough of it, for I had torn my sleeve in one of my excited movements across the railway car to see a view. After mending this I made a sketch of the hills to be seen from the window, and then was driven by hunger to overcome my shyness and look for a meal in the dining-room. A very friendly waitress served me immediately with a supper I shall never forget:

salmon, chicken (with all sorts of small attendant dishes), griddle-cakes with clover honey, and real tea, such as I hadn't enjoyed since leaving home.

The beautiful evening tempted me out for a stroll along the hill-paths and through the pine-wood behind the hotel. Then I sat on the grass and tried to impress the scene on my memory – and succeeded. Everything combined to make it memorable, although each item by itself was familiar – mountains all round and a white mist in the valley, the dark pines, the rising moon, and one brilliant star – such things any one may see. But other items in the scene, equally familiar, gave a unique touch to it. The lovely green and red signal lights I had often admired outside King's Cross station; but here they twinkled like fire-flies. Little mountain trains I had known in Wales, but here great thundering expresses were hurtling through, with enormous funnels, horn-blowing and bell-ringing in the misty valley. One engine-driver's face looked weird in the glow of his fire, and reminded me of the steersman in the most haunting line of the *Ancient Mariner*. It grew dark and I reluctantly went indoors – to find another surprise. Half the floor of the big hall had been cleared for dancing and a string band was playing, interspersed with singing in which the dancers joined. Acutely conscious of my everyday dress, rendered worse by my poor mend of the sleeve and my walk in the wood, I found a secluded chair and hoped to escape notice. I would have gone up to my room had I not found the scene too amusing and the music too intoxicating. Very soon some one came up to me and begged for a dance. I couldn't resist and quickly forgot my dress in that merry and friendly crowd.

The next morning, as I was waiting in the lounge for my train to come up, I noticed parties of young men and girls standing about in groups, all of them equipped for going up the mountains. 'You're not *going*!' they exclaimed. 'You mustn't miss the chance of such a perfect day as this for the mountains.' When I pleaded the shortness of my time before sailing for England, they said, 'But this is the Switzerland of America. Risk missing your boat. Cut Boston short. Come right along with us now.' If ever my mouth watered it did then, but my slender purse had already endured big inroads . . . . The many follies I've committed in life don't cause me half as much regret as the follies I never tasted.

My new train had an observation car at the rear, where the passengers were crowded; but they were most courteous in making room for the new-comer, and in pointing out and naming places of interest. The views of the White Mountains, and especially of Crawford Notch, made me regret still more my not having made the ascent; but I was grateful enough to that conductor who had saved me from passing such delights in the night-train.

A fifteen minutes' stop at a wayside halt doesn't sound pleasant. There was no town near, nor anything. But I have never come across such a dream of a refreshment-room. The bar was loaded with freshly cut sandwiches (not deadly similar within), new buns, an enticing variety of cakes, huge pears, oranges, and jugs of creamy milk. I compared it with our English refreshment-rooms, usually so stale, dirty, and graceless. I understood Dickens's description of the American at Mugby Junction: 'I la'af. I dew. I la'af at yewer fixins, solid and liquid.' More than forty years have passed since I had that wayside meal, and yet an American would still laugh at our rock cakes and coffee essence and other miseries. Dickens's satire had no success in this direction.

I don't think there was any scheduled time for this pleasant stop, but when the conductor thought we had had enough to eat and finished our rambling round the engine and chat with the driver, he said, without raising his voice, 'All aboard,' and we all climbed in.

Glancing at the heading of a fellow passenger's book, I saw 'Sensation in General', guessed it was psychology, and expressed sympathy with her; we then exchanged ideas on teaching, and she told me of a plan being tried in her school for getting children to write quickly; they would copy some simple letter, say *o*, to the tune of 'Bonny Dundee' played on the piano, over and over again without lifting their pens from the page. I still think this is a more useful exercise than the awkward script writing, which is often illegible and never rapid.

It was with real excitement that I jumped out at Boston, found my trunk, and took a hurdy to one of the hotels on Cook's list. A plan of the town was lent me, and I ventured on a short stroll in the hour before dinner. Now the unexpected thing about Boston was that (unlike Canada) it was just what I expected. Indeed, in that first stroll I nearly contributed my bit to the casualty statistics, for I was crossing a seemly looking road, quite naturally endowed with rails, when I was aware of a huge truck towering over me and backing on to me. I skipped off just in time, but returned to the hotel a bit shaken. It was hardly reassuring to read on the notice-board in the entrance-hall that 1,600 cars passed the doors daily – intended as a recommendation.

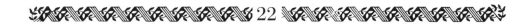

# 22

# MEETING THE SUN

JUST before leaving Boston I had a letter from my late travelling companion warning me of all the dangers of New York. 'On no account take a cab. I had to pay six dollars for mine.' I pictured the scene with some amusement – the cabby's revenge for the many trunks and a haughty manner. I forget the other pitfalls of the city, but thought it would be wise to check my one trunk straight through to the hotel, and so be independent of cabs. My route lay by train to Fall River and thence by boat to New York. It was dark when I went aboard; I was dirty and tired with the train journey, and had to wait ages in a queue to see the purser, to get a state-room. When at last my turn came the only thing left was to share a cabin with five others. One sight of these quarters was enough to keep me from bed as long as possible, and I amused myself by prolonging my dinner and watching my fellow passengers. The *S.S. Plymouth* was said to be the finest of its kind afloat, and it seemed to be used for pleasure trips, for although it looked already full enough, lots more people came aboard at a port where we called; and there followed the gayest scenes of music and dancing in the saloon. Driven by fatigue to my berth I had a miserable night, and when we docked in the morning I felt too weak and faint to get about. Turning resolutely from the inviting cabs, I induced a car to stop for me, and reached the haven of the Broadway Central Hotel. After a bath and breakfast and a couple of hours' sleep I felt equal to anything.

There was no time to waste, for in two days my boat sailed. A little business had to be done first, including a visit to the post-office for letters, and another to Cook's to get my money changed. How pleasing were the English sovereigns and pennies. I kept only enough American money for immediate needs, except one gold piece which I put away carefully (and still possess) as a memento of so jolly a visit. Even these short walks exhausted me, for New York exhibited a kind of heat completely new to me. Boston had been hot, but here there was a dry, choking heat, as though one were being smothered in blankets. I even longed for the Atlantic, and I can't put it more strongly than that. I discarded as many clothes as I could, and understood Sidney Smith's desire to take off his skin and sit in his bones. In addition to the heat the noise of the street was terrific, although the traffic in Broadway was anything but enormous as compared with Oxford Street or Holborn. The paving consisted of those big stones (about the size of an ordinary brick) that used to make travel in the buses of the old days so sickening, and that have now been discarded in London. Some one in the hotel explained to me that the extremes of heat and frost in New York defied any attempt at better paving. But I expect that by now something has been done to counteract the noise.

No more walking that day for me, and I spent the afternoon in a twenty-five cent drive round Central Park, feeling sorry for the Americans that they had not such grand old trees as we have in Kensington Gardens. One road I was particularly anxious to see – Fifth Avenue. This I had always understood to be the home of millionaires and the intellectual and social *élite* of New York. I expected a super-magnificent Park Lane. I went along it, and said to myself, is this really it? No doubt there is more than meets the eye.

And now only one more day in America, and all New York to choose from. I was quite certain what my choice would be. I meant to go to see the Stock Exchange, weather or no. My father had told me little bits about the London Stock Exchange, and I knew that no outsider could enter its holy precincts. To this day I am fond of going down Throgmorton regions and watching all the busy to-ing and fro-ing in the street, picturing my father among them. Well, I understood that the New York exchange was not so exclusive, and that any one might go up into the gallery at Wall Street and look down on the brokers broking. I had heard that they did a good deal of shouting, but the scene exceeded my wildest fancies. The yelling and the gestures were a blend of the lion-house, the monkey-house, and the parrot-house in the Zoo. There was only one other spectator in the gallery, and presently I remarked to him that the citizens of New York were missing a splendid entertainment. He looked at me in a puzzled way, and then said, 'It's new to you. You are a stranger, you're English, aren't you?' I admitted it, and he added, 'Well, we don't think anything of this; they're just doing ordinary business; it's a dull day – a darned slack day. You must come again when there's something really going on.' 'Unfortunately I'm sailing tonight,' I replied, 'so there will be no other chance.' 'Then I hope you have had a good time and seen plenty.' I laughed as I told him that I had only two days for New York, and so far had seen only Central Park, Fifth Avenue, and the Stock Exchange. 'Come with me now,' said he, 'and I will show you as much as possible in ten minutes.' He then took me to the top of the Equitable building, whence there was a view of the whole city. 'You can tell

*Broadway in 1893, pen and ink impression by Molly*

them way back,' said he, 'that you saw *all* of New York.' Unfortunately all I can remember now is the statue of Liberty, which I had already seen sufficiently, but my friend gave me statistics of the number of people who could dine in her head, or something equally absurd. It made my arm ache to look at that statue, and I realized why a piece of sculpture should never give one a restless sensation.

For my last afternoon I went for a stroll, but was careful not to stray too far from my base, lest I should get lost again. Even so, I soon became exhausted with the heat, and thought I would go back on the elevated railroad. Spying a little booking-office I asked for a ticket to the nearest station to my hotel. 'Five cents,' said the clerk, as he slapped down the ticket. Searching my purse I found that I had come out without any small change.

'Sorry,' said I, handing back my ticket, 'I'm afraid I must walk back. I've no money on me except an English sovereign.'

'Oh, do let me look at it!' cried the clerk, and when I handed it to him he gazed on it as in a trance, and then said, 'I'm English, too.'

'What part of England do you come from?' I asked.

'A place called Manchester,' said he. 'Do you know it?'

'Do I know it!' I laughed. 'Why, every one knows Manchester. I'm only a Londoner, and the saying is that what Manchester thinks today London thinks tomorrow.'

He thereupon thrust my sovereign and the ticket back to me, and said it didn't matter about the five cents. We managed to shake hands through the little booking-hole.

I was quite glad to get back into the shelter of the hotel, for the weather had developed a terrifically high wind, a sort of sirocco. I amused myself by making a pen-and-ink drawing of Broadway from the veranda, then packed my hold-all and watched the scenes in the street until dusk, when it was time to start for the boat. My trunk had been sent on, so that I had nothing to do but make my way to the docks by car. Again I had that queer feeling of the unreality of the whole thing – stepping out of an hotel and boarding an Atlantic liner so casually.

The S.S. *New York* was a palatial affair compared to the *Adriatic*. I had a roomy cabin all to myself (an advantage impossible to overrate), and as soon as I had disposed of my things I wandered about to explore the vessel. Presently it occurred to me that it was rather cold-blooded to leave a country where I had been treated so hospitably without saying good-bye to someone. Seeing a young officer, I said, 'Which way is it to the sea, please?' When he laughed, I explained that it was not exactly the sea that I wanted, but to find the place where I could get ashore. Then I ran across the gangway on to America again. It was now quite dark, but not far away I saw the glare of some stalls. I bought two large pears, and astonished the man by telling him that I was all alone, was just off to England, and wanted to say good-bye to him. When I added that I was hungry but couldn't bear to face the ship's dinner, I think he put me down as mentally deficient.

I had been in my berth some time before the tremble of the engines told me that we were off. Determined not to let my nausea keep me in my cabin, as it had done on the outward voyage, I struggled into my clothes each morning and crawled up on deck, so glad to have got past the smell of india-rubber. I made no attempt so much as to look into the dining-saloon. But I had hardly been tucked up in a rug on a deck-chair by kindly fellow passengers before a steward would come along with beef-tea, followed by another with sand-wiches. The weather was splendid, and all the other passengers were bursting with health. They were amused at my lying there all day, and used to stop for a chat as they went by, and tease me. 'One would think you were a mamma instead of a girl!' 'If I had to scrub the deck,' I argued, 'I would probably be well enough to do it; but as I have nothing to do, why shouldn't I do as I like?' Concerts and things were going on in the distance, but they couldn't induce me to attend them; so they brought me several books to beguile the time. Of these I tried three: one described a broken-hearted lover, another a forsaken girl, and the third a mother's death-bed. After these I preferred merely revelling in the idea that I was getting nearer England. Lunch-time made a pleasant interlude. A little while before it was due the steward came to me with the menu for me to make a choice, and then the various things were brought to me on a vast tray, served in a most appetizing way. At some time each day the purser sat down for a chat. He was a charming fellow, full of droll anecdotes, and I began to suspect that pursers were chosen simply for their ability to make the voyage agreeable for the passengers.

What with these many chats, the continual little meals, watching men cleaning the already spotless things on the ship, and the excitement of sometimes seeing a steamer in the distance, the days never hung heavily. I compared them with those endless days on the *Adriatic*, and commented on the difference to the purser. 'But they really *are* shorter,' he exclaimed, 'because we are meeting the sun,' and proceeded to explain it at great length. I agreed to all he said very heartily, for I felt I would rather go west again than be made to understand what happened. 'The upshot of it seems to be,' said I, 'that you lengthen your life by travelling west, and if you kept at it thoroughly there is no reason why you should ever die.' He said there was something in my point, but it obviously set him back a pace, and the subject was fortunately dropped.

On the last evening a specially good dinner was laid out on my tray, with real grapes, so different from those I had eaten in America, which looked and tasted as if they had come off a woman's hat. When I remarked on this to the steward he said, 'Captain's dinner — special.' Whether it was the captain's dinner or a rumour flying round that the Scilly Lights were in view, I can't say, but suddenly my legs returned, my head was no longer giddy, and I ran along the deck waving my arm and crying, 'Hurrah for Cornwall'. To think that Tony and Reskadinnick were just over there! I could hardly sleep that night for excitement, found none of the former difficulty in dressing in the morning, and was early up on deck. I caused a small sensation by going into the dining-saloon for breakfast and eating heartily. 'Whom have we here? A stowaway?' was among the bantering remarks.

Then followed a cheery bustle of good-byes and hopings to meet again, of handing out letters and sending off telegrams. For me there was a long letter

*The Last Evening, by J.J.J. Tissot*

from Arthur, begging me to give Cornwall the go-by and come straight to Wales. Instructions were given about distinguishing the various stations at Southampton, about every possible train I might catch, where to change, and how he would expect a telegram as soon as ever I could give particulars. He would come to Southampton to meet me were it not for the old *res angusta*. In case the letter should go astray the more intimate parts were in Welsh and Latin.

I parted regretfully from my friend the deck-steward. Not knowing what was the correct tip, since no one had been waited on as I had been, I confided to him my difficulty, and offered him all the American notes that remained to me. He demurred to this and asked did I know how much it was. I said no, I wasn't at all clear, but it didn't matter, as I was never likely to go to America again.

I had jumped with glee from the gangway and was looking around in sheer delight at being on English ground again, when an elderly man and a younger one approached me, asked me where I was intending to go and what my luggage was, and offered to arrange everything for me, trains and all. While I was explaining Arthur's directions to the older man the younger one had gone off and soon drove up in an open fly with my trunk aboard. He then took me to the right station for Wales, sent my telegram for me and saw me off. He refused all payment for fly and telegram, and said it was a pleasure. I like to think that these kindly people were not members of some Society for the Protection of Young Females, but were just being helpful to any one bewildered on arrival at a big port.

My train was a rackety old thing, finishing an honourable life no doubt on an unfrequented line. It was one of those soft September mornings when the sleepy countryside looks its best – green fields with overgrown hedges, where the children gathering blackberries stopped to wave at the train . . . old red farms and grey churches. It all reminded me of my mother's saying that England always seemed to her like a garden when she returned from abroad. As we drew near to Winchester I hung out of the window to catch a glimpse of the ancient royal city and the cathedral. In the station the guard strolled up for a word and told me that I was the only passenger. When I said that I had been over to Chicago he was greatly interested, for his wife had a nephew out in those parts, and he felt sure that I must have come across him.

I passed through bits of England that day that I shall probably never see again, for it was an oddly cross-country journey. My first change was at Oxford, where I saw a woman struggling with a child and a lot of luggage. As I helped her along I asked her where she was going. 'Quebec,' said she, 'a terrible long way.' 'It will soon be over,' said I, 'and when you get there it is such a lovely place, something like England, you know. I've just come from there, and I was so sorry to leave it.' This cheered her, and I was able to pack her comfortably in her train before mine came in.

The usual confusion at Shrewsbury seemed quite homely, and the hills of Wales homelier still, and as we slowed down for Machynlleth I saw Arthur at the extreme edge of the platform.

*A Violin*

# 23

# PREPARATIONS

THE year 1896 was humming with preparations for the Queen's coming Jubilee. Arthur and I too were humming a little on our own account. The Golden Jubilee had been the occasion of our first meeting, and we thought it a good idea to be married in the Diamond one. The risk was great, but the future was bound to be uncertain, wait we never so long. Arthur had built up a fair practice at the Bar, and I had saved a nest-egg of two hundred pounds, so, we thought why not? and fixed on 1897 as our second lucky year. Realizing that I should have no more chance, when married, of paying 'bachelor' visits to my brothers, I determined to allot my remaining holidays between them – Christmas with Tom and Easter with Dym. A third visit, an earlier summer one, was thrown in, and it so chanced that these three visits served as a preparation for married life, since they gave me a glimpse of it in three important stages – in the second year, in the tenth year, and in middle age. . . .

It was in the summer that a barrister friend of Arthur's, named James Corner, invited us both to spend a fortnight at his place in Hereford. Holmer Park was a real 'place' in the old-fashioned sense – a mansion in large rambling grounds, with horses and carriages, friendly dogs, and other animals everywhere about. There must be hundreds of such places in England, and I should not mention our visit were it not for the unusual characteristics of the owners. Mr and Mrs Corner were rich and contented. Their one son was now grown up, and they were left alone to enjoy together a delightful middle age. I have come across a few wealthy people and an untold number of jolly people, but this combination of wealth, jollity, and middle age is unique in my experience. The servants of the establishment seemed endless – maids, grooms, gardeners, and odd boys about, all busy over something. But it was Mrs Corner herself who opened the door to us when we drove up from the station; and although we had resplendent meals, there was none of the fussy formality of being over-waited upon that detracts from the fun.

We were taken for long drives in the country, shown the cathedral and other interests of the town, including the old house that had once been the Butchers' Guildhall. Here the carvings amused us, for the sainted bullocks with wings and what looked like haloes gave the impression of the beasts in Revelation. We had lazy afternoons pottering in the garden, the stables, the kennels, and the poultry-runs, or lying in hammocks and reading. New books and periodicals were scattered about untidily everywhere, competing with the dogs for the best chairs. In short, it was a house to delight a man, being at once comfortable and well mauled.

But it was the talk that I enjoyed most. I never can see why 'shop' should be considered boring. I wanted nothing more entertaining than to hear Mr Corner and Arthur discussing their cases and the clever advocacy of Carson and other legal stars of the day. I would hear tantalizing scraps like this: 'My case was quite hopeless, but I saw my little jury.' 'The judge was hesitating . . . he might come down on either side . . . so I gave him a cushion to sit on – a little case on all fours with ours – and he sat.' Both Mrs Corner and I were pleased with one of her husband's stories, because it showed how a woman could outwit men: this female criminal had to be conducted by train to prison in the charge of two police-officers. At a junction there was a change and a short wait, she demanded to be released in order to visit the ladies' room; the two men kept guard outside the waiting-room door; time passed, and they grew anxious about catching their train; on investigation they found that the inner room was connected with the first-class one, and their prisoner had merely walked quietly through and was well away.

When Mrs Corner and I were alone we had many pleasant talks. She had no pretentions to learning or wide reading, but she had acquired a philosophy of life that filtered through to me as she talked. It might have sounded mere common-place had it not been illustrated every hour of the day by her own life; and later on I learnt that she and her husband had had their full share of trouble. 'I'm old enough to give you some advice on married life, dear,' said she, 'and, believe me, to be really happily married is a work of art, just like a painting or a piece of music, and I think myself that it's the greatest of all. Don't be surprised if there are dark shadows too. Surely life without any griefs or worries would be as fatiguing as if there were nothing else, and certainly dull.'

'What do you think,' said I, 'of Dr Johnson's remark when he heard that a married couple had never had a quarrel – "What a damned dull life they must have had!"?'

'Did he say that? Then I don't think much of his wisdom.'

*Torn Lingerie, by Frederick Frieseke*

'I'm so glad you feel like that,' said I, 'for it has always seemed to me neither funny nor true.'

'The wonder to me,' said Mrs Corner, 'is that any one thought it worth preserving. I suppose the old fellow was thinking of those humdrum couples who seem to live like vegetables with no spirit even to be annoyed.'

Encouraged by her views on this subject I then asked her opinion of another thing that had troubled me a little. An uncle's kindly advice had been, 'Be sure you don't expect too much of one another.' This seemed to me such a half-hearted insipid way of starting a great adventure. 'Yes, yes,' broke in Mrs Corner eagerly, 'fancy being cautious all the time, afraid to ask, afraid to give, lest you should be asking too much or giving too much! No, dear, just go headlong at things together, and life will get more splendid at time goes on.'

# WEDDING WITHOUT TEARS

I N the summer of 1897 the whole country seemed given up to gaiety. The 'Queen's weather' of glorious sunshine began to work in the early part of the year and was repeating the glories of 1887. People from all parts were pouring into London, all the public buildings and shops were vying with one another in their decorations, and the coming Jubilee was the main topic of conversation. The lucky owners of windows overlooking the route of the procession were making small fortunes by letting seats.

A seat was quite beyond my means, and I was too old a Londoner to think of jostling among the crowds in the street. But luck, as usual, came my way. My ever-constant friends, M'Jane [Mary-Jane] and Yetta, went to the great expense of hiring two rooms in Cheapside, high up, with windows giving good views of the road. This astonished me, for they were always ostentatious about their radical views, and it seemed inconsistent to pay money merely to watch homage being paid to some one who after all was only a fellow mortal. But at heart they were as conservative as any one, and almost fanatically loyal to the Queen, whose joys and griefs they had always seemed to share. With great forethought they invited some quite young cousins to see the procession, because these would be able to remember such an historical event when they were old. And for no good reason I was asked to share the fun.

And great fun it was. We all started off in two four-wheelers, M'Jane cumbered with two big baskets. We had to arrive early, for the streets were closed to traffic some hours before the ceremony. But there was no dull moment. Cheapside is historic enough when empty, but the overpowering interest now was to watch the increasing crowds getting wedged together and full of good-tempered excitement. Still more amusing was the way in which every available peep-hole in Cheapside had its spectator: roofs, window-sills, some very perilous-looking ledges, and even chimneys. I guessed that Shakespeare must have seen something of the kind, probably in that very road — always the London route for a triumph.

Meanwhile the true inwardness of M'Jane's baskets was appearing. Cold chicken, tongue, and ham she had thoughtfully placed in sandwiches, so that at any exciting moment we could eat them with still an eye on the window. Lemonade, fruit, and chocolate were always within reach. For later in the day (when the procession should be over and there was a wait before we could get away) she had brought spirit-lamp and kettle for a big sit-down tea.

M'Jane preferred to busy herself in such matters rather than look at the crowds too much, for they made her dazzled and nervous. What an ordeal it must be for any one who is the centre of such a crowd, the one on whom all eyes are strained. The Queen was nearly eighty. Since it was considered easier for her to remain in her carriage than to enter the Abbey, as she had done for the former Jubilee, the open space outside the west door of St Paul's was chosen as the site for the service of thanksgiving.

We watchers became aware that this service was over and that the procession had left the cathedral, from the indefinable stirring among the crowds below, very much as one becomes aware of the approach of a train from the behaviour of the people on the platform. The rumour, 'They're coming!' seemed to spread from nowhere. We could see the extra craning of necks and could hear the distant cheering, getting ever louder. Presently Captain Ames appeared. He had been chosen to lead the procession because of his great height and fine bearing. After him came long lines of soldiers and sailors of every kind, and from all parts of the Empire. No such representative procession had ever been seen in England before. As each fresh contingent appeared cheers poured forth. At last a roar of almost alarming strength told us that the Queen was at hand. I had not seen her since the early seventies, when she drove along Essex Road (for some obscure reason) and I had been held up to get a view. I then saw a little lady in black and had been rather disappointed that she looked like anybody else. And now the quarter of a century didn't seem to have made much difference to her. It was the same little lady in black, but now she carried a parasol — a merciful protection not only from the blazing June sunshine but also from the sight of so many people perched in perilous spots. Specially engraved on my memory was her personal escort: on one side of her carriage rode her son, our long-beloved Prince of Wales, and on the other side her grandson, the Kaiser — both of them in resplendent uniforms, mostly white. All the brilliance of her surroundings merely emphasized the majesty of the little lady in black.

In all those rejoicing crowds I was the most joyful, for I was to be married early in July. As Arthur and I walked about the streets that evening to enjoy the decorations we regarded them as celebrations of our own crowning mercy. The only one I remember is the device of the old London and North Western Railway, displaying with greatly enlarged capitals, 'Longest, Noblest, Wisest Reign'.

For our wedding we needed no festivities, for the fact itself was feast enough. Nor did getting married present any dire problem. Our chief wealth was the fewness of our wants. The bits of furniture that we each had acquired for our rooms were almost enough to start with, but we were obliged to find somewhere to put them – somewhere to live. We had plenty of advice in this matter from our friends. One section of them said, 'Be sure you have a house, not a flat, because you will want a bit of garden.' The other section urged the advantages of a flat – 'Easy to manage, easy to leave for holiday-time, and no stairs.' After looking at endless places of both kinds we fixed on a flat in the middle of Ladbroke Grove, said to be 'six-roomed, with kitchen and bathroom'. When we told the agent who was showing it to us that we could count only five rooms, he pointed to a dark cupboard, suitable for storing trunks, and said, 'This is the servant's room.' I record this to show that such conditions were thought possible for a human being in '97. Arthur was so indignant with the man for suggesting such a thing that he was for walking out at once. I argued that there was plenty of room without the cupboard, and we decided to take the flat, for it was by far the best we had seen. Arthur scrutinized the terms of the lease in order to find some objection, but the only one he could discover was our being forbidden to keep pigeons. 'I don't *want* to keep pigeons,' said he, 'and heaven knows I never shall, but I refuse to be told that I mustn't.' So the clause was deleted.

Nothing then remained to be done but to have our various belongings moved to the flat, from Gray's Inn and the Ladies' Chambers, and supplement them with a few necessities. This involved a short gap for each of us to be homeless. Arthur took some furnished rooms in the neighbourhood of the Temple, and I spent the week with Mary Wood, who had long been promised that I should be married from her home in Camden Road. The idea was that our wedding gathering should consist of Mary and her sister Ursula, and our four brothers – two of Arthur's and two of mine. Since these last were all married, Arthur got one of his bachelor legal friends to act as best man. Custom appears to forbid this office being held by a married man, the reason for which only Frazer knows. Of course, Arthur's parson brother, Llewelyn, was to marry us, Tom was to give me away, and the others were just to rally round and cheer us on. I expect most people have such jolly designs for simplicity, and are thwarted by their friends.

*The Heart of the Empire, by Niels Moiler Lund*

The lunch [at Yetta and M'Jane's] was a solemn business, an ordinary midday meal unrelieved by any alcoholic note. Although there were several young cousins around the board, obviously expectant of some fun, I sensed that any levity on my part before the ceremony was misplaced. I was glad when it was over and Mary took me up to a bedroom to 'robe' me, and we could fool about a little in the process. But we felt more solemn when we saw the carriage that Yetta had ordered to take us to the church, and the bow of white ribbon that the driver displayed on his whip. I amused Mary on the way by telling her of Arthur's habit of running everything up to the last moment. 'We shall no doubt see him pelting along Holborn, trying to overtake us.'

As I went down the steps to the church I was overjoyed to see my two brothers, Tom and Dym, grinning a welcome at me. 'Arthur's here all right,' said Dym, 'getting jolly nervous that you won't turn up in time.' Yetta, of course, had gone before me, and as Tom led me up the nave he told me how they had all been amused by her telling him and every one else exactly what they had to do. 'A bit stiff, you know, when it came to informing Llewelyn.' I suppose no woman forgets her last walk in her maiden name, and no woman can have a happier memory of it than I have: on the arm of an ideal brother I was walking to an ideal husband, and as I went was vaguely aware of quite a little congregation of old pupils and students and friends, as well as several of Arthur's barrister friends. Among them I specially noticed, and managed to greet with a smile, Mrs Keyes, in a brightly coloured new bonnet.

Arthur and his best man, Tom and I, with my little bridesmaid behind, were all present and correct – but no Llewelyn. Yetta grew very restive and was actually making a movement to haul him out of the vestry when he bustled forth and began. There had been a great deal of argument in the press as to whether a woman ought to promise to obey her husband, and some brides had omitted the word. So I said my 'obey' firmly, feeling the pleasure of having no longer to order other people's lives, but to be ordered myself. I still seem to feel the grip with which Arthur 'took' me, and the fierce way in which he pressed the ring home. Llewelyn felt it his duty to give us a short address, but as we had had ten years to consider the matter we hardly needed an exhortation as to our duty; the mere idea of Llewelyn in his canonicals solemnly preaching to us struck me as so absurd that I had to fix my attention on the great east window to keep from laughing.

*The Supreme Moment, by E.F. Brewtnall*

# 25

# ORDINARY STRUGGLES

MOST newly married women have the same difficulties to meet: servants or the lack of them; finding good provision shops; keeping expenditure down; making the daily routine run smoothly in the new surroundings. I had my share of all these, and made a fair crop of mistakes.

We returned from Salisbury on the Monday afternoon, and spent the rest of the day in pottering about the flat, putting up pictures, sitting on packing-cases, and revelling in the bare fact of having a home of our own. For supper we went out to a little restaurant. Miss Rogers's present had been a large lamp, and fortunately I had laid in a supply of oil; it was therefore possible for Arthur to sit up and have a last go at his brief for the next day. So it was not till the following morning that my troubles began.

There was no gas in the flat (nor ever was for the seven years we lived in it). Now I had been accustomed to do marvels on the little gas-ring in the Ladies' Chambers – cook porridge, fry bacon, scramble eggs, and even make a stew. And here I was faced with a huge iron range for my first attempt at a breakfast. Disraeli said that there were three things a man should never grumble at because they were unalterable – the weather, his wife, and the kitchen range. But I think he would have let loose a few expressions if he had been in my shoes. I had got up early, lit the fire, filled the kettle, arrayed slices of bacon in the pan, only to be met by smoke billowing forth at me from my 'fire'. In despair I called out to Arthur for help. He just shoved a damper or two about, and that impish range, seeing a man on the job, gave up its tricks and blazed up brightly. I felt that it was like the nursery rhyme 'stick won't beat dog': everything began to hum – kettle began to sing, bacon began to frizzle, cloth was laid, and, best of all, Arthur had been got out of bed in good time.

As soon as he had started for the Temple I was busy enough. Most of my time was spent in unpacking cases, pushing things into place, and tidying away the oceans of packing-paper and straw that surged around. I couldn't make a bonfire, and I didn't dare to irritate my range. I thought of the story, that

*A Maidservant, by Albert Goodwin*

puzzled me as a child, of the old woman whose square house became round; the explanation being that she thrust everything into the corners. Then there was the servant's room to get ready, for she was to come on the following day. I had a rooted idea that a servant's bedroom must have pink chintz covered with muslin round her table. With some trouble I had managed to buy these things beforehand; and now I had but to nail them on to a little table, make up her trestle bed, and lay out her caps and aprons.

A friend had recommended to me a girl of eighteen, from East Dereham, in Norfolk, and I had made arrangements to meet her at the terminus on the following afternoon. I found Emma a fresh-faced, cheerful country girl. She had never before left her village, and told me that she had liked the journey, but had been dreadfully afraid, as the train rushed through several stations, that it wouldn't stop at London. The streets made no impression on her as we drove out to Ladbroke Grove, but she was astonished at the seventy steps that led up to our front door, and quite alarmed at her first venture forth alone: 'I didn't know where that road was going to, mum.' On her second venture she came rushing up the stairs again in great distress: 'I met a funeral, mum. Oh, I couldn't have went. Down hoom it means a death in the family.' As there was a cemetery at the end of the road, I had to kill this superstition at once.

Emma's turns of speech fascinated me, especially the Norfolk idioms. One neat phrase was an absolute 'do', equivalent to the clumsy 'if it should happen'. Thus she would say, 'I hope it won't rain, do we can't go'. She used the word 'deen' for any small quantity, but always in the negative: 'There's not a deen of sugar left' – 'We've not heard a deen of the postman.' She sang, more or less all day long, odd snatches of hymns and popular songs. I was besought at all hours to count my blessings, name them one by one, and told that I should be surprised at what the Lord had done – a bit irritating when the milk had just boiled over. An organ-grinder was one day playing a tune that I failed to recognize, and I asked her what it was. She at once diagnosed it as 'Say Olive Oil'. 'How queer,' said I. 'Why say olive oil? How does it go on?' 'Say olive oil, say not good-bye.' And then, of course, I gathered its meaning from the context. Sometimes of an evening, when Arthur was at work, the singing was trying. 'I shall have to stop it,' said I; but Arthur wouldn't allow that. 'Let her sing while she can,' said he, 'the time may come when she has no heart for it.'

Emma was a treasure. She not only knew how to work, but knew what to work at – a still more valuable asset. For I was ignorant in this line. I had vague ideas that servants were busy all the time, but what they were busy at was a mystery. Emma had a special day for 'turning out' each room, always cleaned the silver on Friday, and devoted Saturday to the kitchen. As for washing, I wished she had kept a special day for that, but she had a penchant for washing, and would wash at all hours. Things that seemed to be spotless would go into the tub if I turned my back. When I protested that the poor towels and pillow-cases were getting done to death by this ruthless washing, she laughed and said 'That's just what Father says, because down hoom Mother is always scrubbing. "If the landlord only knew it," he says, "he'd put five pounds on to the rent for what you take out of the house by for everlasting cleaning it."' I could see that Emma liked me to go out, so that she could get on with her work faster, and surprise me with her results on my return.

I had to leave her alone nearly every morning while I went out to do the shopping. Bessie of Guernsey, of mature experience, had advised me to get everything at Whiteley's. 'You've only got to walk into the shop, order what you want in the different departments, and you find everything delivered at your door.' She was right, but I soon found that this easy way of buying had to be paid for by too high prices, so I determined to explore the neighbourhood, buy what I wanted, and bring it home myself. There were actually some shops on the ground floor of our flat, but not of the right kind. One was a tailor's. But I never saw any symptom of tailoring going on, nor any customer going in. The shop row was one of those in London that seem doomed to failure for no assignable reason. One day Arthur found to his amusement, scrawled in chalk on the pavement, the words 'Lord have mercy upon us'. This was not intentional sarcasm about the shops, but was probably the work of a pious old fellow who used to stride to and fro in Notting Hill and say urgently into one's ear as he passed, 'Do you love Jesus?' I used to answer 'Yes, indeed' to cheer him, for I fear he suffered much from small boys.

One fortunate morning I found, quite a short distance away, another of London's oddities. It was a complete contrast to our row of respectable shops — no outward attractions and yet enjoying the liveliest trade. In an old narrow winding lane, once no doubt a medieval thoroughfare, I found shops and stalls catering for those who have no money to waste and mean to get the utmost value for their outlay. They were not to be put off with stale vegetables or doubtful fish — such as I had experienced in the 'better-class' shops. I expect Bessie would have been shocked to see me coming home with my booty, for, of course, nothing was 'sent up'.

One shop, a greengrocer's, was the most satisfactory place of business I have ever been in, for there seemed to be no waste at all. It had been so successful that it had spread out into an enormous rambling store, and was always

*The Metropolitan Poultry Market, by W.J. Morgan*

crowded with customers. The premises were allowed to remain ramshackle, no books were kept, no credit given, and the whole energy of the staff was devoted to getting the best they could every morning from Covent Garden and selling it quickly at a small profit. By the 'best' I don't mean exotic fruits or anything out of season, but great piles of all that was 'in' – such as fresh strawberries, raspberries, currants – served out to the first comers (often little children) with good humour, homely manners, and very little wrapping up. Once I had already filled my shopping basket when I spied some sprouts and begged for a paper bag to put them in. 'Not for greens, my dear,' was the inexorable reply.

Meat I preferred to buy in another road, for the joints and pieces in the lane were turned over by prospective buyers. But fish was always safe. 'Are those soft roes?' I asked a huge woman who was presiding over a mountain of fresh herrings. 'I won't deceive you, my dear,' said she, 'they ain't.' How she managed to have such an intimate knowledge of every one of them was a puzzle to me, till Arthur explained that the soft roes are sorted out at Billingsgate, as being more valuable. He took great interest in the scraps of experience that I related to him in the evenings. They added to his apparently inexhaustible store of odd information – mostly derived first-hand from contact with the people he met, from judges to tramps. On a railway journey once with a commercial traveller, he entered into the difficulties, disappointments and even tricks of the trade, to such an extent that the man couldn't believe that he hadn't done some 'travelling' himself. This propensity to talk to every one came from sheer interest in life, with no ulterior motive, but, of course, his uncanny acquaintance with a man's daily routine was of great use when a witness was cross-examined, for the unexpected knowledge would surprise a liar into truth.

*Advertisement for the 'Champion' Hand Ice Machine*

# 26

# BRONWEN

WHEN life hums happily along one day seems much the same as another, in retrospect. But an unusual event revivifies the preceding incidents, and the trivialities just before the greatest day of my life stand out as though they had happened yesterday.

One morning in the late spring of '98 I went out to do my usual shopping in Portobello Lane, and captured a fine piece of cod for the evening meal, and some shrimps to make a sauce for it. Then I bought oranges at the famous greengrocer's, where I had on one occasion bought eight good oranges for a penny. The pudding was to be Arthur's favourite, a marmalade one, called Sir William Watkins. This was always a bit of a gamble, but to my relief it turned out finely, and as it was backed up by cheese straws and coffee, all went well. Then we settled down to our usual game of chess. Annoyed at being beaten, though it was my usual fate, I demanded another game and a chance for revenge. No good. So then Arthur settled to his law work and I to my 'parlour work'. We gave this name to any kind of sewing, from a story of my mother's. She had invited an old servant to come to tea, and the reply was: 'Thank you, mum, I'll come when I have a bit of parlour work that I can bring.' When she came she brought a pair of her husband's trousers to mend.

I felt a bit tired and went to bed early, and about half an hour later I tapped on the wall to summon Arthur for a consultation, as I called it. He thought he had better have a second opinion, and ask the doctor to look in. Since the latter lived quite close he was soon on the spot, and dispatched Arthur to fetch the nurse (who, of course, like all nurses, was at another case in some remote suburb). Before starting Arthur called up Emma and told her to light the fire in the special room prepared for the emergency, to get me into it, and to sit with me until he returned with the nurse. Emma was as excited as myself, delighted to speculate with me on all the possibilities ahead, as we chatted away the time in the firelight. Most reluctantly she returned to bed when the nurse arrived, at two o'clock.

Even at that forbidding hour the energetic little nurse felt that she ought to be doing something or asking where something was. I understood the expression 'snatches of sleep', for all I got that night was really snatched from a running fire of questions, washings, combings, and straightenings. A spread of small bustling surrounded the nurse like an aura. All this was at least cheerful and even funny, but what I found hard to bear was being kissed in a repetitive way, like a duck at its dinner.

At this point, like the Baker, 'I skip forty years'. It seemed like years, for it was not till eleven o'clock next morning that my first-born appeared. The doctor was very kind; he guessed that I had never had such a long and hard spell of work before. 'Now you understand,' said he, 'the full force of the word "labour".' At this I told him of a German governess I knew who greatly admired the Litany. 'It prays for every one, even the poor governess.' I was puzzled, and asked which petition she meant. 'For all women labouring of child,' she replied. (By the way, it was this linguist who thought that 'Keep to the left' on our street shelters meant 'Asylum for those left behind.')

Perhaps there may be some greater peaks of happiness for mortals, but I have not heard of anything that could come up to the joy of that morning. It compensated to overflowing for all the trials and difficulties of our ten long years of waiting. And it was a girl that Arthur had been secretly longing for. How swiftly and quietly he came along the passage, afraid to shout or laugh or touch or come too near . . . putting all his energy into rubbing his hands and gazing at this marvel. The babies I had so far seen were little wrinkled, crumpled things, dull red all over, but this was a lovely creature, pink and white, and smooth as a shell. I remembered how my mother used to describe her astonishment at the beautiful face of her second boy – quite unlike the others of us; so I concluded that this vision might actually be my own child and not some heavenly changeling.

Arthur had much difficulty in tearing himself away to the Temple, but got home 'brave and early', as the Cornish say. 'We had a celebration,' said he, 'champagne at the "Cock"; and I've been sending telegrams like mad. And I've put a notice in *The Times*. Atkin advised this, for he says you get more than the money's-worth in gifts from advertising firms.'

And so we did. To Emma's delight every post for several days brought some exotic soap or baby-powder, some patent food or delicate ointment, and a photographer sent us even a photograph of the notice in the paper.

Arthur was so wrapped up in his daughter that his friends in the Temple teased him a little and accused him once (to his shameless delight) of carrying a bottle of milk in his brief-bag. 'Of course I do,' he replied, 'one mustn't be unprepared, one never knows, and I have a serious job on – I'm founding a dynasty.' One evening as he was brooding over his new possession he said, 'You know I shall be fined for this?' And he explained that when they were on circuit any man who had had a stroke of luck was always fined; there were other strange old customs – for instance, at dinner during his first circuit he was asked which he would have, Old Testament or New. Not knowing what it meant he said, 'Old', as it sounded more solid. And so it was, for he had to drink right off a tumblerful of port. The New would have been only claret. As for the impending fine, I suggested that he shouldn't mention his daughter at all. 'A sound piece of advice,' said he, and laughed.

It was a grand time for me. My room was gay with violets and daffodils, letters of congratulation poured upon me, as well as presents of food dainties, little garments, cot accessories, and so on. My brothers, Tom and Dym, were vociferous in their pleasure at my having achieved a 'lil maid' (to quote Tom's Cornish term of endearment). Neither Arthur nor I had a sister, and my brothers' children were all boys, so that a girl in the family was something of an event. A letter that I valued very much came from Mrs Ruck, of Pantlludw; after hearty congratulations she added: 'Ask Arthur to repeat to you a Welsh proverb which says, "It's wise in having children to have a girl first."' She ended with a strong wish to hear the new friend's name as soon as it was settled.

'Well, what about her name?' said Arthur as we read this, for we hadn't discussed the matter at all.

'She is Welsh,' said I, 'and there is no doubt what her name must be. She is Bronwen.'

'Do you really mean that?' exclaimed Arthur, glowing with pleasure. The name of his old home in Wales was Fronwen, which means 'the shining hill', and the corresponding name for a girl is Bronwen, which means 'the shining breast'. I felt sure, from the way he used to speak it, that this name made him love her still more.

The great moment of the day was seven o'clock, when Arthur was due to come home. There was no music in the world like the sound of his latch-key. His first words never varied when I went to greet him: 'How is she?' Not that there was ever anything the matter with her; but there was always some new accomplishment to relate – a smile, a palpable smile; what *looks* like a tooth coming; an attempt to pull herself up; an enlargement of the appetite; and, of course, an

*A Saturday Afternoon, Arthur and Bronwen, from a pencil sketch by Molly*

extraordinary intelligence, for which 'taking notice' was a feeble word.

On Saturday afternoons we hoped there would be no visitors or anything at all to disturb Arthur in his complete enjoyment of Bronwen's company. He had bought a kind of weighing machine for recording her progress in pounds and ounces. For this ceremony she was put in one half of my Japanese basket, but it wobbled about so much that I placed no confidence in the weight that was registered. But my arms told me she was getting on.

Yes, Saturday afternoon was the great time for us all. After a short outing, Arthur would settle himself in his deep old basket chair and have Bronwen on his knee. I took my parlour-work and Emma made any excuse she could to hover in and out. Bronwen's idea of sport was to tug her father's moustache till he cried 'Ooh!' Then she took to giving a proleptic 'Ooh'! herself, just before a specially hard tug. Toys had been given her in plenty but she took to none of them, sometimes hurling them out of her pram or into her bath. What she liked best was to play with anything that we ourselves were using or wearing. I had brought from Switzerland a brooch with a tiny cow-bell attached, and this she loved to ring. Some optimist had given Arthur a sovereign-purse, which he wore on his watch-chain to inspire confidence; this she would contrive to squeeze into her mouth as she sat on his lap. One afternoon she had become excited with some of these games, and I heard Arthur say, 'Here, Emma, take her; there are ominous sounds.' Ever after that Emma used to refer delicately to 'omnibus sounds'. Sometimes Arthur would play a dance tune for her on his fiddle, while she would joggle up and down to it on my lap, and when it came to bed-time he would lull her to sleep with Gwynedd Gwyn. It had for long been his dream to have a daughter who should play the harp, and any pleasure she showed in sounds was a happy omen. Baby-talk he never used to her, but would chat freely to her of this and that, sometimes even appearing to be asking her opinion on some legal point. No doubt he interpreted her gay gurgles quite usefully. One night, in the small hours, she began crying for an extra meal, and continued her demands while I was getting it ready, drawing forth a sleepy protest from Arthur: 'Bronwen, your complaint is not based on the necessity of the situation.'

The great event in the spring of 1899 was Bronwen's birthday. As Arthur was leaving in the morning he gave her a toss in his arms and exclaimed, 'One year old! You are now riding on your two, as the Welsh say.' He promised to be sure to come home for tea.

I was expecting quite a birthday party. Mary Wood was unable to come, but sent a white silk frock for her god-daughter to look grand for the occasion. One of my Cornish cousins and an old college friend came with gifts of shoes. M'Jane and Yetta brought a large ball for Bronwen to roll about, and a blue silk sash to add to her white frock. With them came an old lady friend of theirs and, most valuable of all, a cousin, an eight-year-old boy. This little Wilfred laid aside his dignity, abandoned himself to the situation, and crawled about the floor with Bronwen. He not only chased the ball with her as though it were the one end in life, but also he made circles with his arms and arches with his legs for her to crawl through to reach the ball, which she managed with crows of triumph.

This was my first serious tea-party, and it seemed quite a cheerful company with no lack of conversation. On the material side I had endeavoured to make it as grand as possible, with wedding-presents at last given a chance to be shown off. On a wooden tray, carved for me by Miss Russell, the secretary of Bedford College, I had laid out the blue tea-service given me by M'Jane. A home-made cake, and some more reliable bought ones, I had displayed on a table given me by Mrs Bryant. These various objects provided more talk when it was most required, for one of the wedding-presents was creating a hold-up;

this was an extremely ornamental brass kettle on a tall tripod stand, with a minute methylated spirit-lamp poised in the middle. It was the first occasion that had been important enough for its use, and I may add that it was the last. However, it had one advantage – it afforded great pleasure to Yetta, who knew exactly how to manage it, and took over the duty. Even under her control it looked like being a long time before the thing would actually come to the boil, so I slid out into the kitchen to engineer a preliminary pot of tea in order to set things going. Here I found Emma in a great state of agitation. I had sent her out to get some cream at a dairy close by. 'Look mum,' she cried, 'what they've charged me a shilling for! Why, down hoom it would have been tuppence.'

The tea was poured out and cream added when Arthur breezed in, just in time to help Wilfred hand round the things. He felt obliged to remark that the birthday cake was a bit sad in the middle, but M'Jane immediately insisted that the best cakes are always sad in the middle. She also remarked when Bronwen's white silk frock showed signs of devaluation from the floor exercise, 'Never mind, Molly, it will wash like a rag.' One would like to have M'Jane behind one at the Day of Judgement.

After this first milestone Bronwen forged ahead faster than ever. She could walk about by pushing a little chair in front of her. She would spring in my arms with gleeful cries of 'Mum, Mum', and welcome her father with 'Dad, Dad'. Her favourite word was 'up', the most expressive, I suppose, in the whole language, for joy or sorrow, life or death – we wake up and we break up. Often I heard Bronwen muttering it softly to herself before attempting the adventure; then she would pull herself upright to chair or couch and exclaim aloud 'UP', as triumphant as one who has achieved the Matterhorn.

Mary Wood's sister Ursula was then specializing in portraits, and suggested that she should do an oil-colour of Bronwen sitting in her high chair. This idea was particularly pleasing to Arthur, for his main vision of her was the little person thus seated at breakfast, 'chatting' to him in her own way. The portrait was a big business, necessitating several visits, and I wondered how Ursula managed it at all, for a lively baby can't pose, and has to be caught; but it turned out a great success.

The last days of May were upon us, and the warm spring sunshine was penetrating the flat, making us think of the coming summer and our long-promised visit to Cornwall, when we could show Bronwen to Tony, who would be sure to spoil her as she had spoilt all of us.

One evening my old headmistress and friend, Miss Bennett, came over to see us. Whether it was the effect of the baby or not I can't say, but she seemed to

*The Kitchen, by Duncan Grant*

have shed her extreme propriety and to be as humanly foolish as our other visitors. She pronounced Bronwen to be the picture of health, and I said, 'She has not had an hour's illness since she was born.' It was pleasant to note that Miss Bennett lapsed, as we all do at times, into our ancient paganism. 'Oh, don't say that,' she immediately rejoined, 'you know how the Greeks felt that the gods are jealous of human happiness, and if they hear people boasting . . .' She broke off with a merry laugh and shake of the head.

It was two mornings later that I noticed a new accomplishment in the little creature lying in her cot by my side. She was gurgling to herself, and waving her little hands about, as though keeping time to some tune she had made. As I watched, the sound changed to something like a moan, and I soothed her to sleep in my arms. We were troubled to see that she hadn't her usual appetite for breakfast, and made no objection to being laid in her cot again. Arthur was distressed out of all proportion to such a slight indisposition; said he had a case in court or would stop at home; he would look in at the doctor's as he went by, to send him along; and I must be sure to send a wire if things were the least bit worse.

The doctor came at once, and thought there was a little stomach trouble; I was to give no food, but watch very carefully and send for him again if things didn't improve. I kept her in my arms all day, and she slept a little and smiled now and again, so that I felt hopeful that the trouble was passing. But at about four o'clock, when I thought she might swallow a little warm milk, she suddenly threw back her little head and began to gasp, and then to my horror she became unconscious. I told Emma to fetch the doctor, and then to go on to the post office and wire to the Temple, 'Come home as early as you can'. I made her repeat the message very carefully. There was no need to tell the poor girl to hurry. Half distracted when alone with the little one I made my way to the bookcase, found Yetta's book of advice, and with one hand managed to see what to do in case of a fit – a hot bath was suggested. I went to the kitchen again but could do nothing about it till Emma's return. At last she appeared. The doctor was out, but would come as soon as he returned. In her anxiety she had wired the words to Arthur, 'Come at once'. This added to my anguish, for I knew how such a message would turn his heart to water. I ought to have remembered that whenever he was in a tight place all his wits were quickened, and that he would never spend an ounce of energy in mere emotion that might be useful in action. He did not come at once. Instead of that he tore round to his brother Alfred and brought him along with him. He also wired to Yetta, knowing her to be practical as well as ever ready to help. She was one of the governors of the London Hospital, and she wired for a nurse to be sent to me post-haste.

I pass over hurriedly, although I can recall them only too vividly, the details of those dreadful hours, as the fight for the little life went on. The fit passed off, consciousness returned, and there came the blissful sound, the familiar little 'Mum, Mum'. It was a chance that did redeem all sorrows that ever I had felt.

The doctor and Alfred hung over the cot, with the nurse attending, keeping on with various spongings to keep the temperature down. Arthur and I stood by in the background. After hours of watching Alfred whispered something to Arthur, and I was asked to go and fetch some necessity – I forget what. Only too thankful to be able to do something I went into the dining-room to find the thing required. I had barely got there when Arthur followed me into the room, shut the door, took me in his arms and dropped his head on my shoulder with the words: 'Let her go.'

The supreme phases of our life here – love and birth and death – each has the power of breaking down the barrier between us. We glory in the first two, in spite of their attendant pain. Why don't we acknowledge the majestic strength of the last? In that moment of anguish Arthur and I were one as we had never been before. But our poor human frames crack under the pain, and I hope I may never again see a man broken down with grief.

Since writing this short record I have realized the number of empty hearts that Bronwen filled with warmth and joy. And she did her little stroke all unawares . . . 'dear childe.'

*Emma with Bronwen and her Doll, from a pencil sketch by Molly*

# 27

# THREE SONS

URING the following years three boys came to cheer us. Our natural anxiety about the health of the first gradually lessened as he got over every little ailment, and when his two brothers grew strong and lively our cares were thrown to the winds.

Life was so full of things to be done every moment that there was hardly room for worry to take root. Money was never plentiful, and we were glad to add a little to our coffer by some simple literary work. Through Mr Corner's influence Arthur was given the job of writing the London Letter for the *Herefordshire Times* once a week. I was proud to be able to contribute a paragraph to this now and again, and I also wrote an occasional article for an educational paper, and did a great many reviews. All this made a pleasant change from domestic duties. I can give no orderly account of those strenuous years, but pull from my memory a few happenings that stand out, not for their importance, but for some oddity.

Londoners who live in flats are more distant with one another, if that is possible, than next-door neighbours. This is, no doubt, from the fear that the proximity would be unbearable if relations became at all strained. In the flat below us there came to live a young married couple, and after a while I ventured to call. I was well received, and as we chatted I learnt that a baby was expected. I immediately offered to lend the trestle-bed I had bought for my nurse, and a few other appurtenances that were now lying idle. At this the lady drew herself up and looked at me queerly, obviously suspecting me of some sinister motive. 'But,' said she, 'why should you, a perfect stranger, lend me these things?' I replied that I was an old Londoner and knew that such an offer from a neighbour was *ultra vires*, but that I was also a Cornish woman, and accustomed to a different code. Then we both laughed and became friends. So much so indeed that later on, when she was in difficulties after her nurse had left, I was actually allowed to go down and bath the baby for her. She little knew what delight it was to me to have such a task again.

That friendship was the only *rapprochement* afforded by the neighbour-

*Lordship Lane Station, Dulwich, by Camille Pissarro*

hood as such. We had endless visits from old friends, from relations passing through London, from my old schoolfellows, and from any friends of theirs who were within hail. But from mere neighbours, not one. There were several churches close by, but no clergyman called on us. People in flats are regarded as birds of passage, no doubt, devoid of souls, although we stayed seven years, and strange to say my friend below is still in her flat with husband and daughter.

One child in a flat is all right, but when we had two boys we felt that more space was wanted, and a bit of garden. We consulted Bradshaw to find some spot that was 'country' and yet provided with a few fast trains to town. Barnet filled the bill, and was specially attractive to me for its associations with my father and brothers, who used to take long walks from it as a base. The very name pleased me, as reminiscent of my brother Barnholt.

In those days Barnet was very different from what it is today. There were no trams, and the only bus was a little one-horse affair that plied between New and High Barnet – continually to be seen, but never on the spot when wanted. Where now you see road after road of new prim villas, of latest design, we enjoyed spacious open fields, country lanes, with over-hanging hedges, and enticing foot-paths. Our house was an old one, overlooking a park with a large pond and great spreading trees. A gate at the bottom of our garden led into the grounds of our landlord, a kindly old fellow who loved the company of one of our small boys as he pottered among his fruit trees and vegetables.

Kindly, yes, and so was every one else. Accustomed all my life to the aloofness of Londoners I was amazed at the immediate friendliness of the Barnet people. The vicar came quite soon, and of course a doctor was necessary when our third boy arrived. Both the vicar's wife and the doctor's wife were of that charmingly indiscreet type that is the despair of their husbands and the joy of their neighbours.

Another rich vein of friendship was the railway journey to town. Arthur was soon one of a coterie who took the same express every morning. He went third-class, but it was soon usual for some of the richer business men to forsake their first-class carriage and join those whose purses were lighter and conversation brighter.

What with the vicar and the doctor, our quite contingent neighbours, and the wives of Arthur's train companions, I soon had plenty of friends. Paying calls, however, was not in my line, and I found it expedient to build up a character for eccentricity.

'You promised to come and see me,' said a friend I met in the road, 'but you have never been.'

'Ah,' said I, 'but then I never meant what I said. What I like is for people to drop in on me just when they feel inclined and never expect me to call on them.'

She was too astonished to be offended, and fell in pleasantly with the idea. So did many others, and hardly a day passed without some one popping in, to exchange notes about a cookery recipe, to play with the boys, or join in with anything we were doing.

The days were full enough, for although I had a servant for housework I never had a nurse. This was not so much from lack of means as from my preference for looking after the boys myself. There was no kindergarten at hand, and even if there had been one I should not have cared to send them to it. Kindergartens are fine institutions, but those I had seen gave me the impression of too much dainty attention to the children, too much absorption in their important work on the part of the teachers, too much of the 'Isn't he sweet?' and 'Isn't she a darling?' My ideal was more of a rough-and-tumble environment. A married servant of my mother's said to her once, in solemn tones, 'You know, mum, children *thrive* in the dirt.' Mother perceived the big principle underlying this statement, and determined that her own children should be perfectly clean once a day, and beyond that might get as dirty as they liked.

Our new surroundings were splendid for such an ideal. There was an attic at the top of the house for the boys' own, to set out their train lines, build with their bricks, and romp as they liked. There was a garden to grub in and trees to climb. I didn't want to make them nervous, and I hope it will be counted to me for righteousness that when I heard a 'Hullo, Mother!' from the top branches of the fir, or saw a boy walking along the perilous edge of the garden wall, I went indoors to suffer in silence, often muttering to myself Hagar's 'Let me not see the child die'.

Not far away was a pond, containing minnows and stickle-backs, and one afternoon a little figure appeared slung about with every appliance for catching them and a glass jar for bringing them home. 'I'm going fishing, Mother,' he announced. 'Won't you have your tea before you go?' I asked. 'No; fishermen do not care to eat.' The right spirit, I thought.

Casualties were frequent to both bodies and garments, but nothing serious. Falls downstairs, grazed knees, cut fingers, and bruises were little accounted of. A great triangular tear in knickerbockers would be shown me, with 'It won-matter, will it, Mother? It'll soon mend, won't it?' In such a case as this I found one of my neighbourly visitors extremely useful. 'Oh, do let me mend it, Mrs

*Advertisement for Brooke's Soap*

Hughes,' and of course I hadn't the heart to refuse her.

Materials of all kinds were in constant demand for operations in the attic. String, empty bobbins, pieces of wood, bits of cloth, sheets of brown paper — but commonest of all was the query, 'Have you got a box, Mother?' 'What size do you want?' 'Oh, just a box.' I have not yet cured myself of hoarding every box that comes to the house.

Naturally I tried to give the boys some serious teaching, and soon found that very little actual sitting down to it was required. At least on my part. Each boy, after reaching the responsible age of four, was set down to some morning task. But any reasonable outside demand was permitted. Thus, one morning the second boy was a very long time coming home after seeing his father off at the station. 'Where have you been?' said I, for he looked rather the worse for wear, although radiant. 'I been delivering with Payne,' was the proud reply. Payne was our greengrocer, and the little chap had been staggering to people's doors with greens and potatoes. I guessed that he had learnt as much in that way as in his 'lessons' at home.

These lessons chiefly consisted in the boys doing something by themselves while I was busy in the kitchen. Results or difficulties were brought to me wherever I happened to be. Drawing of some kind was the basis of nearly everything. Thus for starting reading I had made a packet of cards, drawn an object on each and printed its name below; so the word (as it would look in a book) became familiar long before the separate letters were distinguished. Then it could be copied,and there was the beginning of writing. The transition to real reading was made easy through Mary Wood, who brought something to help me every time she came. Among her gifts were two books of priceless value. The story of *Little Black Sambo* was read aloud to the boys, soon known by heart, acted in the garden, and then read by themselves — such words as 'beautiful' and 'umbrella' (impossible to teach on any rational system) being soon recognized in any context. The other book was a little folk's edition of *Alice in Wonderland*. By the time that these, and *Peter Rabbit*, were mastered there was no more anxious bother about reading. I have seen countless books of 'systems' for teaching children to read, and have come to the conclusion that the only thing is to give them a book (with some good illustrations) containing a story that they *want* to know.

In spite of Mr Harding's warning I followed his ideas about the beginnings of arithmetic. With the boys' assistance I painted red spots on postcards, arranged as on playing-cards, so that a five, a six, a seven, and so on could be quickly intuited. A few of these would be dealt out and added up, such words as twenty, thirty, and forty coming as happily surprising new words. One day the glad news was reported to me in the kitchen, 'Mother, I've got to *tenty*!' That was the moment to acquire the new word 'hundred'.

Quite another aid to realizing number and size came in an unexpected way. The gift of a very large box of plain bricks gave endless pleasure for building purposes. The well-made pieces of hard wood varied in size from a cubic inch to lengths of ten inches, adapting themselves to being railway lines or men-of-war with rising decks or houses or temples, while the little cubes could pose as people. It was only as I watched the play that I perceived their further value. 'Hand me a six,' one busy builder would cry. 'Can't find a six, will a four and a two do?' The actual handling of the different sizes seemed to me valuable, and I encouraged a pride in putting all the bricks in the box before bed, for the mere fitting in had its advantages. The boys are now scattered far and wide, but those bricks are still intact.

I don't know whether the love of measurement is common in children, but the boys seemed to have a passion for it, and the eldest enjoyed even angles and the use of a protractor. I told him one day to draw any number of triangles he liked, all shapes and sizes; then to measure the angles in each very carefully and to add the results. I went about my own business, and after a long time came the surprised report: 'It's so funny, Mother, they all come out the same!'

Occasionally it was one of the boys who set a problem to me, and I was not always equal to it. One day I was at the sink washing up the tea-things, when the youngest approached with, 'Mother, who *is* the Holy Ghost?' I confess that I temporized: 'I'm busy just now, darling, but another time . . .' He ran off contented and forgot his difficulty. Another day the middle boy, chancing to be out with me alone, asked me what electricity was. Here I felt on surer ground, and enlarged on the subject at some length, not a little pleased at the silent attention of my audience. I was rewarded with, 'Oh well, when Dad comes home I'll ask him, and he'll splain it properly.'

Arthur had plenty of explanations to make, for my knowledge of mathematics or engineering was never regarded as reliable. It was the early days of motor-cars, and they were rare enough for us to make a game of counting them on the Great North road; one boy kept a little note-book for recording their numbers. On one grand afternoon we had the bliss of seeing King Edward go by. On another hardly less exciting occasion we saw an aeroplane over our fields for the first time. It used to delight me to see Arthur with one boy on his knee, and the other two hanging on his shoulders, while he drew diagrams and explained what the inside of a locomotive was busy about, what the different wheels of a watch were for, how a motor-car worked, and how a plane managed to get up.

In the matter of geography I was sketchy, being content with getting the boys to know where important places were, and to be fond of maps. With the aid of picture postcards we got on fairly well. The counties of England and Wales, and the countries of Europe were learnt without trouble by means of puzzles, sensibly made so that each county or country was a separate piece. I would hear, 'What's become of Devon? It's that nice fat one,' or 'Find Northampton for me; it's a long one.' Rutland was troublesome, in constant danger of being lost.

As for grammar I was on velvet. When I had books to review there had fallen into my hands *The Child's Picture Grammar*, a gem by Rosamund Praeger, gloriously illustrated in colour. In most schools there is much agony inflicted on teachers and taught by trying to cope, in junior classes, with case and gender, voice, mood, and tense – many of them things that the English language has wisely thrown off. All that a healthy child needs to know is the business of each part of speech. Now this book depicted them in anthropomorphic style, with comic illustrations and a story, so that they became personal friends of the boys. The page on pronouns showed two boys fighting, while their grown-up nouns were having a rest. They had got confused as to which noun they each represented. In this way the useful slogan was learnt – 'One pronoun, one job'.

Unless the weather was absolutely forbidding, every afternoon was spent in a walk. Hadley Woods provided a glorious playground for exploring glades, climbing, jumping, hiding, gathering blackberries, collecting chestnuts, or watching the various kinds of trains going by on the Great Northern. But we had a walk to and from the woods through rather dull streets. The youngest boy was in and out of a mail-cart, and quite content, but the other two were bored on the way out and tired on the way back. So to ease the situation I used to tell stories, on the true Chaucerian model. As may be supposed, I was frequently gravelled for matter. To 'tell a story' in an isolated way is difficult when the demand is continual. A verse of Keats came to my mind – 'All lovely tales that we have heard or read, an endless fountain of immortal drink' – I began to explore the various sources of good tales that I knew, and found them indeed endless. To save the bother of selection I assigned a different day to each source: thus, on Mondays I told a Bible story, on Tuesdays a story from

*Boy Studying, by Peter Vilhelm Ilsted*

English history, on Wednesdays one from Roman history, on Thursdays one from the *Iliad* or *Odyssey*, and on Fridays a fairy story or a Norsk legend or a fable from Aesop. Of course I had to enlarge and embroider to make the stories last out. I remember taking the length of Station Road to describe the gorgeous home of the rich young ruler – his horses, his grand dinners, his purple clothes, his apes and peacocks (these last borrowed from Solomon). The boys saw that it was no light thing to give up all these jolly things to go and help among the very grubby poor people that he could see around Jesus. It was after some such story that the middle boy said, 'What happens to us when we die, Mother?' 'Nobody knows,' I replied. 'Ah,' said he 'I expect Jesus is keeping it secret, so that we shall have a nice little surprise.'

I suppose to children there are few things to equal the pleasure of surprise, especially the surprise of an unopened parcel. Christmas was the grand time for this, when every present was put away until the appointed moment. It was a day or two before this feast when the middle boy said to me, 'I hope you will die on Christmas Day, Mother.' 'Well,' said I, 'it's not very likely that I shall, why do you want me to?' 'I want to see the blood coming out.' 'Oh, but you know people often die without the blood coming out, you can't rely on it.' 'Oh well, then, never mind, don't bother about it.'

Of course, the boys had many picture books, and no doubt made up strange stories for themselves from them. Their father arrived one Saturday afternoon with an enormous volume of Hogarth. He had picked it up at a sale and had great trouble in dragging its weight home to the door. It is only when I am in extremely high spirits that I can bear to look at those terrible satires. I was surprised to find how often the youngest boy demanded to have it put on the floor for him, and would apparently revel in it. Idly one day I said, 'Which picture do you like best?' He said at once, 'Oh this one, Mother,' and turned to Hogarth's realistic depiction of a man being drawn and quartered.

Home-made picture books provided a useful pastime. I got some blank scrap-books, and the boys pasted into them any odd pictures they could collect. One book was kept for history, another for geography, and another for illustrations of the Bible. All this involved much cutting and messing with gum. The house was never very tidy. One morning a neighbour looked in and expressed astonishment at finding me busily engaged in putting everything to rights. 'I read in the paper yesterday,' said I, 'about a woman who was murdered, and it said that the police found her cupboards and drawers in great disorder. So I thought I had better tidy up a bit, in case I get murdered.' 'Don't you worry,' said my kindly neighbour, 'the drawers will all get untidy again before you are murdered.'

*Arthur's old friend Bourne, who had emigrated to South Africa, brought his family to stay with the Hughes. Their daughter, Hilda, was a special favourite.*

'What a darling little girl she is,' said Arthur to me when our visitors had gone, 'how I wish that our boys were better behaved. I feel quite ashamed when

I see other children so polite and obedient – their cousins, for instance, how good they are.'

'Yes, of course they are,' said I. 'When their favourite uncle comes to see them they are gracious hosts, and when they come here they are gracious guests. No father ever really sees other people's children. Let's hope they're naughty enough in the bosom of their own family.'

'Hope? Why should we hope they are naughty?'

'Well, if children always did exactly as they were told, were always unthinkingly obedient, how could the world advance? And how dull it would be. Tell me now, did you ever do anything really bad when you were a boy?'

'I often used to go blind with rage.'

'That's all right. It's better to have a temper to curb than to have none at all.'

'But sometimes it was ugly enough. Once when Llewelyn was asked to a party and I wasn't, I filled his boots with water. It's nothing to laugh at, I've always been ashamed of it.'

'Anything else?'

'Well, once I played truant from our little school. Off I started to get a whole long time to myself fishing in our stream at Corris. It was just the day for it – fish rising beautifully, and I got some fine trout.'

I noticed as he spoke that his eyes were shining at the recollection of that day, and I added, 'There you are! An act of insubordination and a joy for ever.'

*The Three Boys in 1918, by Ursula Wood*